my **revision** notes

AQA AS/A-level

POLITICS

UK POLITICS

Rowena Hammal and
Simon Lemieux

HODDER
EDUCATION
AN HACHETTE UK COMPANY

Orders: please contact Hachette UK Distribution, Hely Hutchinson Centre, Milton Road, Didcot, Oxfordshire, OX11 7HH. Telephone: (44) 01235 827827. Email education@hachette.co.uk Lines are open from 9 a.m. to 5 p.m., Monday to Friday. You can also order through our website: www.hoddereducation.co.uk

ISBN: 978 1 5104 4765 3

© Rowena Hammal and Simon Lemieux 2019

First published in 2019 by
Hodder Education,
An Hachette UK Company
Carmelite House
50 Victoria Embankment
London EC4Y 0DZ

www.hoddereducation.co.uk

Impression number   10   9   8   7   6   5
Year   2023   2022   2021

Cover photograph: Helmut Niklas/Stockadobe.com

Typeset by Integra Software Services Pvt. Ltd., Pondicherry, India

Printed in India

A catalogue record for this title is available from the British Library.

Get the most from this book

Everyone has to decide his or her own revision strategy, but it is essential to review your work, learn it and test your understanding. These Revision Notes will help you to do that in a planned way, topic by topic. Use this book as the cornerstone of your revision and don't hesitate to write in it — personalise your notes and check your progress by ticking off each section as you revise.

Tick to track your progress

Use the revision planner on pages 4 and 5 to plan your revision, topic by topic. Tick each box when you have:

- revised and understood a topic
- tested yourself
- practised the exam questions and gone online to check your answers and complete the quick quizzes

You can also keep track of your revision by ticking off each topic heading in the book. You may find it helpful to add your own notes as you work through each topic.

Features to help you succeed

Exam tips

Expert tips are given throughout the book to help you polish your exam technique in order to maximise your chances in the exam.

Typical mistakes

The authors identify the typical mistakes candidates make and explain how you can avoid them.

Now test yourself

These short, knowledge-based questions provide the first step in testing your learning. Answers are at the back of the book.

Key words

Clear, concise definitions of essential key words are provided where they first appear.

Revision activities

These activities will help you to understand each topic in an interactive way.

Exam practice

Practice exam questions are provided for each topic. Use them to consolidate your revision and practise your exam skills. Note that 25-mark A-level exam practice questions can also be used for AS practice questions.

Summaries

The summaries provide a quick-check bullet list for each topic.

Online

Go online to check your answers to the exam questions and try out the extra quick quizzes at **www.hoddereducation.co.uk/ myrevisionnotesdownloads/**

My revision planner

The government of the UK

REVISED   TESTED   EXAM READY

The politics of the UK

REVISED   TESTED   EXAM READY

Now test yourself answers

Exam practice answers and quick quizzes at
www.hoddereducation.co.uk/myrevisionnotesdownloads

Countdown to my exams

6–8 weeks to go

- Start by looking at the specification — make sure you know exactly what material you need to revise and the style of the examination. Use the revision planner on pages 4 and 5 to familiarise yourself with the topics.
- Organise your notes, making sure you have covered everything on the specification. The revision planner will help you to group your notes into topics.
- Work out a realistic revision plan that will allow you time for relaxation. Set aside days and times for all the subjects that you need to study, and stick to your timetable.
- Set yourself sensible targets. Break your revision down into focused sessions of around 40 minutes, divided by breaks. These Revision Notes organise the basic facts into short, memorable sections to make revising easier.

REVISED ☐

2–6 weeks to go

- Read through the relevant sections of this book and refer to the exam tips, summaries, typical mistakes and key words. Tick off the topics as you feel confident about them. Highlight those topics you find difficult and look at them again in detail.
- Test your understanding of each topic by working through the 'Now test yourself' questions and 'Revision activities' in the book. Look up the answers at the back of the book.
- Make a note of any problem areas as you revise, and ask your teacher to go over these in class.
- Look at past papers. They are one of the best ways to revise and practise your exam skills. Write or prepare planned answers to the exam practice questions provided in this book. Check your answers online at **www.hoddereducation.co.uk/ myrevisionnotesdownloads**.
- Try different revision methods. For example, you can make notes using mind maps, spider diagrams or flashcards.
- Track your progress using the revision planner and give yourself a reward when you have achieved your target.

REVISED ☐

One week to go

- Try to fit in at least one more timed practice of an entire past paper and seek feedback from your teacher, comparing your work closely with the mark scheme.
- Check the revision planner to make sure you haven't missed out any topics. Brush up on any areas of difficulty by talking them over with a friend or getting help from your teacher.
- Attend any revision classes put on by your teacher. Remember, he or she is an expert at preparing people for examinations.

REVISED ☐

The day before the examination

- Flick through these Revision Notes for useful reminders — for example, the exam tips, typical mistakes and key words.
- Check the time and place of your examination.
- Make sure you have everything you need — extra pens and pencils, tissues, a watch, bottled water, sweets.
- Allow some time to relax and have an early night to ensure you are fresh and alert for the examinations.

REVISED ☐

1 The nature and sources of the British constitution

Key points

- A constitution is essentially the rulebook by which a country is governed. It sets out the various powers and responsibilities of each branch of government, as well as laying out the rights and civil liberties of all citizens.
- Constitutions come in all shapes and sizes. Authoritarian dictatorships such as North Korea and the former Soviet Union, as well as Western democracies, have constitutions.

The nature and sources of the British constitution

Nature

Every country's constitution has its own unique characteristics and origins, and Britain is no exception. Table 1.1 identifies the key terms that define the British constitution.

Table 1.1 Defining the British constitution

Key term	Definition and key facts	Significance
Uncodified	• The British constitution is found in a variety of sources, meaning it is uncodified. • Few other countries have an uncodified constitution. Those that do include Saudi Arabia and New Zealand.	• It can make it more difficult for British subjects to understand their rights and how their political system works. • It can make it easier to adapt, e.g. by Acts of Parliament, as no complicated procedures are required to amend it.
Unitary	• All power ultimately derives from central government. • This is the opposite of a federal constitution (e.g. the USA).	• The Westminster Parliament is sovereign and therefore very powerful. • Any power given to the regions (e.g. through devolution) is delegated, not transferred permanently.
Rule of law	• Everyone is equally subject to the laws of the land. • Even governments and ministers cannot break their own laws. • Described by A. V. Dicey as one of the 'twin pillars' of the constitution. • The opposite of arbitrary government, which is commonly associated with dictatorships.	• Identifies Britain as a modern liberal democracy. • Ensures the powers of government are limited. • If a government or minister is found to have broken their own rules or guidelines, they are deemed to have acted *ultra vires*, i.e. beyond the power of the law. • It can lead to the government having to reverse an action, e.g. in 2016 the government was found by the courts to have acted illegally by trying to restrict legal aid to people born outside the UK.

→

Key term	Definition and key facts	Significance
Parliamentary sovereignty	• Parliament is the supreme authority in the land; the constitution is what parliament says it is, and can be altered at will by statute law. • This contrasts with countries such as the USA, which are said to embody constitutional sovereignty where government and legislature must follow the constitution when passing laws. No such requirement exists in Britain. Parliamentary sovereignty is the other of A. V. Dicey's 'twin pillars'.	• This is a fundamental principle of the British constitution. • It means it is flexible and easy to change, as all it takes is for parliament to pass a law to change the constitution. • No parliament can bind its successor, meaning that the constitution is changed and even reversed over time. • Shown by laws both to join the EU originally and subsequently to leave it.

Typical mistake

Students often write that the British constitution is unwritten, but this is not true. Rather, it is uncodified, and found written down in various sources.

Exam tip

Although it is absolutely right to say that the British constitution as a whole is uncodified, some parts of it have been 'micro codified'. For example, the Equality Act 2010 brought together and thus codified several existing pieces of anti-discrimination laws such as the Equal Pay Act 1970 and the Disability Discrimination Act 1995.

Parliamentary sovereignty
The basis of the UK constitution. Parliament is the supreme authority in Britain. This means that parliament's laws cannot be struck down by a higher authority.

Sources

REVISED

As mentioned above, the British constitution derives from several sources, as shown in Table 1.2.

Table 1.2 The sources of the British constitution

Source	Definition and key facts	Significance
Statute law	• Acts of Parliament that affect and alter the British constitution. They can cover laws about who can vote such as the Great Reform Act 1832 and how elections are run (the Ballot Act 1872). • It covers laws that impact on civil liberties and **human rights** such as the Human Rights Act 1998, which incorporated the European Convention on Human Rights (ECHR) into UK law.	• The British constitution remains flexible and adaptable. • The trend has been towards expanding and protecting democracy and individual rights, e.g. giving all women the vote by 1928. • In theory, these rights could be removed or diluted if parliament so desired. In reality, many currently have the 'double lock' of additional backing from EU law or the ECHR.
Common law	• Laws passed down over the years by legal judgements in the courts. • Represents judicial precedence. Examples include the right to free expression and the defence of property rights. • Some key historical documents such as Magna Carta are based on common law not statute law.	• Does not have precedence over statute law/Acts of Parliament. • Statute law can repeal or modify rights granted under common law. For example, although the rights of property owners can be found in various ancient documents, statute laws — such as those dealing with compulsory purchase orders — modify these ancient rights.

Source	Definition and key facts	Significance
Royal prerogative	<ul><li>The historic political powers of the monarch now effectively transferred to the prime minister.</li><li>As an example, although technically the armed forces are those of the monarch, in reality decisions about deployment and size are made by the government not the sovereign.</li></ul>	<ul><li>It is often cited as a way governments can extend their powers, e.g. honours including peerages can be handed out by the prime minister alone.</li><li>It can be limited by Acts of Parliament, e.g. the Fixed-term Parliaments Act 2011.</li></ul>
Conventions	<ul><li>Unwritten traditions that help to 'oil the wheels' of state, and enable government and political activity to run more smoothly.</li><li>A good example is the 1945 Salisbury-Addison Convention whereby the Lords agreed not to delay policies contained in the governing party's **manifesto**.</li></ul>	<ul><li>These normally work well, e.g. they enabled David Cameron to have the first chance to form a coalition government after the indecisive result of the 2010 general election.</li><li>Conventions are not protected by anything more substantial than tradition. If a convention is to work properly, there must be a shared understanding of what it means. A contested convention is not a convention at all.</li><li>When the Lords rejected the People's Budget in 1909 and broke convention, a constitutional crisis took place.</li></ul>
Authoritative opinions	<ul><li>The writings and books of constitutional experts that clarify and explain the inner workings of the constitution.</li><li>Examples include A. V. Dicey's *Law of the Constitution* and Walter Bagehot's *The English Constitution*.</li><li>Also comprise more recent sources such as the Cabinet Manual (2010) which set out the main laws, rules and conventions affecting the conduct and operation of the government.</li></ul>	<ul><li>Authoritative opinions are rather like conventions and have no absolute legal authority but nonetheless help the smooth running of government.</li><li>Not usually approved formally by parliament and can be easily changed.</li><li>Embody and describe existing rules and conventions, and do not seek to change them.</li><li>A good example is when Bagehot made the famous distinction between the 'dignified' and the 'efficient' parts of the constitution.</li></ul>

Human rights Those rights that apply to all people. They are absolute, universal and fundamental. They cannot be removed from anyone.

Royal prerogative The powers traditionally held by the monarch but now, in practice, the preserve of the prime minister. These include the power of patronage, being commander-in-chief and negotiating treaties with foreign powers.

Manifesto A list of policy commitments released by a party before an election. Once elected, a government should deliver its manifesto.

Historic milestones

Magna Carta (1215)

REVISED ☐

- An agreement between King John and his barons that established the principle that everyone including the king was subject to the law.
- Above all, it established the principle of the right to a fair trial.

- Although re-issued and partly altered in the following decades, Magna Carta is nonetheless seen as a landmark document in the development of human rights. Some clauses have found their way into other key documents such as the American Bill of Rights (1791) and the Universal Declaration of Human Rights (1948).
- Note that Magna Carta did not give many rights to ordinary people.

Bill of Rights (1689)

REVISED

- Another agreement between the king and parliament.
- Stated that parliaments must meet frequently, elections must be free and there must be complete freedom of speech within parliament — known as **parliamentary privilege**.
- Also included the principle of no taxation without parliament's agreement.
- Effectively created and embodied the notion of parliamentary sovereignty.

> **Parliamentary privilege**
> The right of MPs to free speech within the Palace of Westminster. They cannot be sued for slander or contempt of court. This is significant as it is considered vital so that MPs are able to do their jobs properly and to speak freely.

> **Typical mistake**
> Don't confuse the Bill of Rights (1689) with later human rights legislation. The 1689 Act was really about asserting the power of parliament over the monarchy, not about key individual rights. Elections might well have been required to be free and fair, but most people did not have the vote in 1689.

Act of Settlement (1701)

REVISED

- Only Protestants, not Roman Catholics, could become the monarch or be married to the monarch, which guaranteed the Protestant succession.
- Its constitutional importance lies not in its anti-Catholic bias, but rather in what it said about the relative power of Crown and parliament.
- Asserted parliament's dominant position since direct hereditary succession was decreed less significant than religious affiliation.
- Established the fundamental principle that the monarchy existed on parliament's terms, not vice versa.

Parliament Acts (1911 and 1949)

REVISED

- Significantly reduced the rights and powers of the unelected House of Lords.
- The 1911 Act removed their power of absolute veto over legislation and limited their power to that of a 2-year delay.
- The 1949 Act reduced the delay to just 1 year.
- Both Acts increased the powers of the Commons over the House of Lords.

European Communities Act (1972)

REVISED

- Brought in by the Conservative government of Edward Heath and marked the entry of the UK into what is now the EU.
- Constitutionally it represented a weakening of parliamentary sovereignty as all British law had to conform and comply with EU law.
- Among areas it impacts are the ability of the government to control immigration from other EU countries and to make trade deals with non-EU countries.

- The 2016 Brexit vote shows how this major impact on the constitution can be unravelled.
- Although the original Act weakened the rights of parliament to pass its own laws, subsequent events have enabled parliamentary sovereignty to come to the fore again. What a parliament in 1972 created, a twenty-first-century parliament can unmake!

Now test yourself

TESTED

1 Why does the Brexit vote highlight parliamentary sovereignty?
2 The Bill of Rights established what important principle dealing with MPs' freedom of speech?
3 Since 1949, what is the maximum length of time the Lords can delay a bill for?
4 What document sets out how governments today should run?
5 Does a convention have legal backing?
6 What are the three features of a human right?

Answers on p. 109

Developments since 1997

Recent developments

REVISED

The British constitution has evolved and developed over the centuries. Major reforms in the nineteenth and early twentieth centuries expanded who could vote and changed the conduct of elections; more recent changes have focused on strengthening individual and collective rights, and the country's relationship with the European Union. There have been some lesser changes to parliament itself and to the power of the prime minister. Tony Blair's Labour government, which was first elected in 1997, made constitutional reform a major part of their legislative agenda.

Among recent developments of the constitution are:

- the creation and expansion of powers in the devolved assemblies/ parliaments in Scotland, Wales and Northern Ireland such as the Wales Act 2014 and the Scotland Act 2016
- a major reform in the composition of the House of Lords in 1999, with the removal of most hereditary **peers** leaving just 92 in place
- the Human Rights Act 1998
- laws that enhance individual rights such as the Freedom of Information Act 2000, the Data Protection Act 1998 and its successor, the General Data Protection Regulation 2018, and the Fixed-term Parliaments Act 2011
- the European Union (Withdrawal) Act 2018

> **Typical mistake**
>
> Don't confuse EU law and the European Convention on Human Rights (ECHR). The ECHR refers to general rights such as the right to a family life. It stems from Britain's membership of the Council of Europe, a completely separate body to the EU. Although a country must be in the Council of Europe to join the EU, a country not in the EU (e.g. Norway) can belong to the Council of Europe and must also abide by the ECHR. The Human Rights Act 1998 incorporated the ECHR into British law and is unaffected by Brexit.

> **Peers** Members of the House of Lords, mostly life peers who have been nominated by political leaders over the years, along with 92 hereditary peers and 26 Church of England bishops.

Significance of recent developments

REVISED

Freedom of Information Act 2000

This Act requires public bodies such as government departments, local authorities and the NHS to:

- publish and make publicly available certain information about their activities such as an annual report and minutes of meetings

- allow members of the public to request information from these public authorities via a freedom of information (FOI) request

The Act is designed to promote openness and transparency among public bodies that benefit from taxpayers' money. It is also meant to boost public trust in such organisations and remove shrouds of secrecy. Its workings are overseen by the independent Information Commissioner's Office (ICO).

Some strengths and weaknesses of the Freedom of Information Act are given in Table 1.3.

Table 1.3 Strengths and weaknesses of the Freedom of Information Act

Strengths	Weaknesses
• FOI requests are popular and widespread; over 45,000 such requests were made in 2016 alone. • It allows the public and **pressure groups** to identify possible examples of waste and inefficiency or, at worst, corruption in public bodies. • It is an important investigative tool for journalists, prising open information that those in power might prefer to remain hidden. For example, the Act played a significant role in uncovering the **MPs**' expenses scandal in 2009. Also, a request by the *Manchester Evening News* revealed that the BBC spent over £110,000 on free tea and coffee at its Manchester offices in a single year. • It allows public scrutiny of policy initiatives and how well they work in practice. For example, in 2006 there was a highly publicised knife amnesty. An FOI request forced the publication of a report into the impact of the amnesty by the Metropolitan Police. This showed it had minimal impact on the rates of knife-related crime. • Those initially denied access to the requested information can appeal to the ICO. There were 461 such appeals in 2016.	• Public bodies can and often do refuse requests for information. This can be for a variety of reasons including national security, commercial sensitivity, cost or because the request is deemed 'vexatious'. • In 2016, 37% of all requests were declined and for 14% of requests only part of the information was released. • It is often the case that requests for information are declined because they would involve the release of private or personal information about individuals. The Act can therefore lead to a conflict between an individual's right to privacy and the right of the public to gain access to information about public officials.

Pressure groups Organisations that campaign for a specific cause, such as a trade union or an environmental campaign group. Unlike a political party, pressure groups generally do not aim to win political power through elections.

MPs Members of Parliament, each representing a geographical area of the UK known as a constituency (650 in total), who sit in the House of Commons. The average number of voters per MP is 68,000, although the largest constituency, the Isle of Wight, has around 105,000 voters.

Exam tip

If you are answering a question about the significance of any one or two constitutional changes after 1997, make sure that you do not just describe the change but also analyse it: how well has it worked and what are its strengths and drawbacks?

Fixed-term Parliaments Act 2011

- Passed following the formation of the Coalition government between the Conservatives and Liberal Democrats after the 2010 general election.
- Weakened the power of the prime minister to call a snap election by dissolving parliament unilaterally.
- Parliament now needs to vote by a two-thirds majority to call an early general election. Alternatively, if there is a vote of no confidence in the government, this must be confirmed by another vote within 2 weeks.

- Designed to enhance the stability of a potentially fragile coalition government and reduce the scope for the prime minister to gain political advantage from going to the polls when the chances of victory seem highest.

The Act's significance has been debated, as shown in Table 1.4.

Table 1.4 Strengths and weaknesses of the Fixed-term Parliaments Act

Strengths	Weaknesses
• It allowed the Coalition government to work well in a stable and effective manner over its full 5-year term. This political stability in turn was seen as beneficial for economic growth and longer-term policy making. • It is fairer on the junior member of the coalition (e.g. the Liberal Democrats after the 2010 general election), as they would not have to face an early election over which they had no say in timing.	• Prime Minister Theresa May did exactly what the Act was designed to avoid by calling a snap election in 2017 within 2 years of the previous election, when polls showed a Tory lead of around 20%. The Commons passed the motion to dissolve parliament on a vote of 522 to 13. • The Act was only passed in the first place because of political circumstances and expediency, not out of high principles. Had it not been for the need to provide stability to the Coalition government, it is unlikely such an Act would have been passed. • It could also be argued that it even failed in its political aim to protect the Liberal Democrats who, after the full 5 years in coalition, crashed from 57 MPs to just 9 in 2015.

Now test yourself

TESTED

7 Whose power was limited by the Fixed-term Parliaments Act?
8 To whom do you make a freedom of information request?
9 What percentage of FOI requests were denied in 2016?
10 What did the Human Rights Act 1998 incorporate into British law?
11 Which institution was partially reformed in 1999?
12 Look at the following developments in the British constitution and identify which Act or historical document provided that right.

Key right or development	The Act/historical document granting it, with the date
(a) Elections should be free and fair	
(b) The unelected chamber in parliament cannot veto laws	
(c) The monarchy only exists on parliament's terms	
(d) The prime minister cannot call an election when it best suits them politically	
(e) Everyone is equal under the law	
(f) An individual or pressure group has the right to find out reasonable details about government departments and public bodies	

Answers on p. 109

The extent of rights in the UK

How well does the British constitution defend citizens' rights?

REVISED

There is much debate over how well the British constitution fulfils this role, as shown in Table 1.5.

Table 1.5 Does the British constitution defend citizens' rights?

No	Yes
● Many laws have loopholes and gaps and can be ineffective (e.g. the 2018 furore over unequal pay for many female journalists at the BBC). FOI requests are often refused.	● Over time, especially through statute laws, more and more rights have been explicitly defended such as the right to access information from public bodies and through anti-discrimination laws.
● The uncodified nature of the constitution means people are unaware of their rights, unlike in the USA where fundamental rights (such as the right to free expression) are enshrined in the constitution, especially the Bill of Rights.	● Codification would not add anything substantial or meaningful to enhancing awareness of individual or collective rights.
● Because of parliamentary sovereignty, no rights are **entrenched or inalienable**.	● Large numbers of people use the courts to assert their rights and demand access to information held about them and by public bodies.
● Parliament could, in theory, repeal or change laws and citizens would be powerless to stop this.	● 'A constitution should be judged by how it works, not by how it looks.' Although possible in theory, in practice this is extremely unlikely to happen. It would take a very extremist government to enact such legislation.
● With Brexit, the 'double lock' of reinforcement by EU law/the ECHR will be lost, making citizens' rights more vulnerable.	● The electorate is unlikely to vote for MPs who will take away their fundamental rights. Even if Britain were to withdraw from the ECHR (itself very unlikely), it is inconceivable that the main and universally agreed rights would not be protected by a British Bill of Rights.

Defending individual and collective rights

REVISED

Individual rights are those that apply to individual citizens, such as the right to free expression, the right to be able to access information held about you or the right to a free education up to the age of 18. Collective rights are those that protect a whole group of individuals; this could include workers in specific jobs, religious groups or disabled people. Individual and collective rights sometimes clash, as shown in Table 1.6.

Entrenched or inalienable
Describes something that cannot be taken away, such as a US citizen's rights in their constitution to equal protection under the law.

Table 1.6 How individual and collective rights might clash

Individual rights	Collective rights
The individual right to privacy.	People suspected of involvement in terrorism or other serious crimes might have their phone calls monitored to protect the collective right to security.
The individual right not to be discriminated against, for example on the grounds of sexuality.	The collective right of religious groups to express and live out their beliefs.
The individual right to free speech.	The collective right of a particular group such as Muslims not to be subject to abuse and hatred.
The individual right of employees not to be coerced or intimidated by others into taking industrial action.	The collective right of workers to be treated fairly and to go on strike if necessary.
The individual right, even for a celebrity or public figure, to keep their private life private.	The collective right of a free press.

Now test yourself

13 Look at the following examples and decide whether each one is primarily about individual or collective rights, briefly explaining why.

Example	An individual or collective right	Reasons
(a) A Christian owner of a bed and breakfast establishment refuses to allow a gay couple to rent a room with a double bed		
(b) Workers for the taxi firm Uber demand to have full employment rights		
(c) A tabloid newspaper finds out a Premier League footballer is having an affair and wants to publish the story		
(d) An employee with mobility problems asks their firm to locate them in a ground floor office as there are no lifts in the listed building		
(e) A group of parents demand that their children's school changes its uniform policy to allow girls to wear trousers		

Answers on p. 109

Summary

You should now have an understanding of:
- what a constitution is and the key terms and characteristics of the British constitution
- the main sources of the British constitution and key features of each one
- the main historical milestones in the development of the British constitution and how they impacted on its evolution
- two examples of constitutional change since 1997 and their relative importance
- how well the British constitution defends individual rights
- what the difference is between individual and collective rights, and how and why they can sometimes conflict with each other

Exam practice

AS

1 Explain, with examples, the difference between a codified and an uncodified constitution. [6]
2 'The British constitution provides few safeguards against the abuse of citizens' rights.' Analyse and evaluate this statement. [25]

A-level

3 Explain and analyse three key developments of the British constitution before 1900. [9]
4 'Statute law is the best defender of citizens' rights in the UK.' Analyse and evaluate this statement. [25]

Answers and quick quiz 1 online

2 The structure and role of parliament

Key points

- The UK Parliament is made up of two chambers: the House of Commons and the House of Lords.
  - The House of Commons comprises 650 MPs directly elected at least every 5 years. The Commons is the dominant house as the 1911 and 1949 Parliament Acts severely limited the powers of the Lords.
  - The House of Lords contains around 800 members. Most are life peers, although 92 hereditary peers remain. There are also 26 senior Church of England bishops.
- Parliament also contains the **executive**, i.e. all government ministers including the prime minister are either MPs (most) or peers. There is no separation of powers as in the USA.

> **Executive** The government, comprising all ministers and led by the prime minister.

The Commons, Lords and executive

Functions

REVISED

Parliament is the main law-passing body in the UK, although certain legislative powers are delegated to the devolved assemblies in Scotland, Wales and Northern Ireland. In reality, most laws are actually drawn up by the government and 'rubber-stamped' by parliament after debates and votes.

One of parliament's key functions is to scrutinise and check the government, though how well and how independently it does this is a matter for debate. Parliament is also a forum for representation, both geographic (via constituencies) and political (nearly all MPs belong to a political party).

Westminster in London is important as a place of national debate, especially in times of national emergency or crisis. Increasingly, a lot of the work of parliament is done in committees rather than in the main debating chambers. The Parliament in Westminster still dominates the UK political process despite devolution, not least since national **referendums** are used infrequently.

> **Referendums** Direct votes in which the entire electorate is invited to vote on a single political proposal. This may result in the adoption of a new law. In the UK, they are normally used only for major constitutional issues such as EU membership (2016) or changing the electoral system to the Alternative Vote (2011).

> **Exam tip**
>
> Be cautious when describing parliament as a law-making body; in reality, aside from private members' bills, most laws are drawn up in advance by the government.

The scrutiny of the executive

How does parliament scrutinise the government?

REVISED

The scrutiny of the executive means checking that the government is carrying out its functions properly. Are its policies working well, is it spending taxpayers' money wisely, how competent and well-informed are ministers? Parliament scrutinises the executive in a number of ways:

- MPs and peers can ask questions, both written and oral, of government ministers. The best-known example is Prime Minister's Questions (PMQs), which are held at noon on Wednesdays for half an hour.
- Debates in both chambers allow MPs and peers to air their views about government actions and policies.
- Departmental select committees investigate and scrutinise actions by civil servants and ministers in each government department, often holding hearings where they can summon witnesses for questioning.
- Bills go through various stages in parliament, often giving a chance for MPs and peers to suggest changes (amendments) to proposed laws. The committee stage (undertaken by public bill committees) gives an opportunity, away from the main chamber, to go through draft legislation more carefully, clause by clause.
- Parliament has the final say in all new legislation.
- A vote of no confidence by the Commons can bring down a government, although this is rare as most governments command a reliable majority in the Commons. The last successful such vote was in March 1979 when James Callaghan's Labour government lost by just one vote.

How effectively parliament scrutinises the executive is considered in Table 2.1.

> **Typical mistake**
>
> Don't confuse public bill committees and departmental select committees. Public bill committees are temporary and exist only for the specific bill they are scrutinising. Select committees are permanent and have a brief to provide wider oversight of government departments and their actions. They do not scrutinise individual pieces of legislation.

Table 2.1 How effective is the scrutiny function of parliament?

Method of scrutiny	Advantages	Disadvantages
Prime Minister's Questions (PMQs)	• They can give positive publicity to the questioner/**opposition** parties, as when Tony Blair famously accused the then prime minister John Major in January 1997 of being 'Weak, weak, weak'. • They allow unwelcome questions to be asked of the prime minister and ministers and can expose weaknesses, such as when the then prime minister Gordon Brown accidentally said: 'We not only saved the world' when he meant 'saved the banks' during a PMQs exchange. • They keep prime ministers and ministers on their toes. Tony Blair once recalled PMQs as 'the most nerve-racking, discombobulating, nail-biting, bowel-moving, terror-inspiring, courage-draining experience in my prime ministerial life'.	• They can convey an image of rowdiness and theatricals: 'an exchange of pointless and useless declamations' according to former Labour MP Gerald Kaufman. • In 2014, Speaker John Bercow wrote to party leaders asking them to help moderate behaviour at PMQs, referring to the atmosphere as often 'very male, very testosterone-fuelled and, in the worst cases, of yobbery and public school twittishness'. • Most questions are designed to either catch out the opposition or praise one's own party.
Parliamentary debates	• They allow free expression of views and opinions about issues of the day. • They are televised so the public can watch and be informed. This improves the accessibility and transparency of parliament. • They are an opportunity to change how MPs and peers might vote.	• Most debates are set-piece occasions; MPs usually adopt the 'party line'. Many use their speeches to impress their party leadership and further their own career prospects. • Few minds and votes are changed by words spoken in the chamber. Most MPs usually vote along party lines.

→

Method of scrutiny	Advantages	Disadvantages
Select committees	<ul><li>They are less partisan and confrontational than debates and questions in the main chamber.</li><li>They are often chaired by MPs from the opposition parties. Yvette Cooper (Labour) chairs the Home Affairs Select Committee. The powerful Public Accounts Committee, which scrutinises value for money across departments, is traditionally chaired by a senior opposition **backbencher** (Meg Hillier in 2018).</li><li>They can call witnesses both from government and outside Westminster to give evidence.</li><li>The government must respond to reports within 60 days.</li><li>Reports are often hard-hitting and influential. For example, in May 2018 the Health Select Committee recommended a number of measures to reduce child obesity. Within a month, the government announced further measures such as stopping the sale of sweets and fatty snacks at supermarket checkouts.</li></ul>	<ul><li>The governing party always has a majority on each committee.</li><li>Consensus between parties is not always reached, leading to majority and minority reports along party lines.</li><li>Witnesses can be evasive and elusive.</li><li>Governments can and do ignore the findings in select committee reports. They only have to respond to and not enact recommendations. For example, in February 2018 the Digital, Culture, Media and Sport Select Committee recommended against the appointment of Baroness Stowell as head of the Charity Commission, but Culture Secretary Matt Hancock went ahead and appointed her regardless.</li></ul>
Scrutiny of draft legislation and voting on the final bill	<ul><li>Enables bills to be properly checked, amended and discussed.</li><li>Parliament can reject the final bill.</li></ul>	<ul><li>Strong party loyalty and discipline mean a government bill stands little chance of failing.</li><li>The governing party has a majority on each public bill committee, so any changes to bills will be minor.</li></ul>
Vote of no confidence	<ul><li>The 'nuclear option', which can bring down a government.</li></ul>	<ul><li>Very unlikely to succeed. Only an unstable minority government would be vulnerable. Even the most rebellious MP will be loyal in such a vote.</li></ul>

Opposition MPs and peers not from the governing party or parties. The term 'official opposition' applies specifically to the largest single opposition party. It has its own frontbench shadow cabinet who directly mirror and challenge government ministers, especially at PMQs. Since 1945 the official opposition has always been either the Labour or Conservative parties.

Backbencher An 'ordinary' MP who is not a government minister or in the shadow cabinet.

Now test yourself

TESTED

1 How many MPs are there in the Commons?
2 What religious group does the Lords contain?
3 Is parliament best described as law-making or law-passing?
4 What is the difference between a select committee and a public bill committee?
5 What must a government do with a select committee report?
6 Who often chairs select committees?
7 What is the chief criticism often levelled at Prime Minister's Questions?
8 Why is a vote of no confidence termed the 'nuclear option'?

Answers on p. 109

Parliamentary debate and the legislative process

Parliamentary debate

Parliamentary debates are one of the main ways MPs, especially those on the opposition benches, get to scrutinise and challenge government policies and bills. They also provide an opportunity for the opposition to say how they would handle matters differently and project the image of a 'government in waiting'.

The topics for debate are largely selected by the governing party, but 20 days a year are set aside for opposition parties to choose the subject to be debated. These are known as 'opposition days'.

Most bills in parliament get debated at the second reading stage (see Table 2.2).

The legislative process

A bill is a proposal for a new law or a proposal to change an existing law, presented for debate in parliament. A bill can start in the House of Commons or the House of Lords and must pass through the same stages in both houses until it receives **royal assent** and formally becomes an Act (law). Nearly all government bills will be successful, especially if they are key manifesto pledges. Backbench MPs have the opportunity to introduce their own bills (private members' bills), but these normally rely on government backing if they are to become law.

Main categories

Public bills are measures that are universally applicable to all people and organisations. The vast majority of **legislation** comes under this category.

Private bills are usually promoted by organisations including councils and private businesses to give themselves powers beyond, or in conflict with, existing laws. Private bills only change the law for specific individuals or organisations, not the general public. The New Southgate Cemetery Act 2017 is a recent example.

Government bills are created and promoted by the government, often to fulfil manifesto promises. All members of the governing party would be expected to support such bills.

Private members' bills are public bills independently introduced by backbench MPs or peers, either as Ten-Minute Rule bills or by being selected as one of 20 'winners' in the annual ballot. Few private members' bills actually become law due to limited time available for debate — only 8 out of 540 between February 2011 and February 2018. Those that do are either non-controversial or receive government backing.

Key stages

The key stages in the passage of a bill through parliament are shown in Table 2.2.

> **Royal assent** The formal approval by the monarch of a bill that has successfully passed through parliament that makes the bill into law. No monarch has refused royal assent since 1707.
>
> **Legislation** The term for all bills that have successfully gone through parliament. A law or Act of Parliament starts off as a bill and only becomes legislation when it has received royal assent.

> **Typical mistake**
>
> Don't confuse private bills and private members' bills. They are not the same thing. Private members' bills are also public bills.

Table 2.2 Key stages in the legislative process

Stage	Importance and significance
First reading	The bill is formally introduced to parliament. There is no opportunity for debate or a vote.
Second reading	The main opportunity for debate, questions and voting on the general principles of a bill. Amendments can also be proposed and voted on.
	Sometimes, governments can face defeats at this stage. In December 2017, the Commons voted by 309 to 305 to give parliament the final say on the final Brexit deal.
Committee stage	A chance to go over the bill and any amendments made in the second reading stage. Each bill is given its own public bill committee comprised of backbench MPs who go over all the clauses in the bill.
	Major changes are rare as the governing party always has a majority in the committee, but small changes to wording can improve the bill's quality. Pressure groups and individual MPs can submit evidence and address the committee at this stage.
Report stage	Any changes made at the committee stage are discussed and voted on. This is the last chance for MPs to propose further amendments.
Third reading	A short debate. No further changes can be introduced at this stage. A final vote on the bill takes place before it goes for royal assent, provided it has passed through the full stages in both houses.
Consideration of amendments	Each house considers the other's amendments before the bill goes to the sovereign for royal assent.

The Lords

The Lords has a key role in revising and amending legislation and can act as a check on the Commons and government. However, the Commons always has the final say. The Lords is best described perhaps as the 'think again' chamber.

Most bills begin their parliamentary life in the Commons and then go through the same process in the Lords. A few government bills are, however, introduced in the Lords first. These are usually non-controversial such as the Automated and Electric Vehicles Bill introduced in the Lords in January 2018.

It is rare for the Lords to reject a bill outright; if they do, the Parliament Act is invoked and the bill automatically becomes law after a year. The Lords can and do make amendments to bills, which are subsequently debated and voted on in the Commons. This often results in bills going back and forth between the two chambers in their final stage — a process informally called 'parliamentary ping-pong'. By itself, the act of delay often causes the government to change course or, on rare occasions, to abandon its plans entirely.

The Lords also has an important function in scrutinising secondary and EU legislation which the Commons often lacks the time to do effectively.

Now test yourself

TESTED

9 How important is royal assent in a bill becoming law?
10 At what stage in the legislative process is a bill most likely to fail?
11 Which stage in the legislative process is described below?
   (a) The best chance to suggest major amendments to a bill.
   (b) The final stage of a bill's progress before becoming law.
   (c) The best opportunity for MPs and interest groups to lobby for specific changes.
   (d) The final vote on a bill.
   (e) When amendments are reviewed and voted upon.

Answers on p. 109

Theories of representation in parliament

The Burkean or trustee model

REVISED

This model is associated with the view of Edmund Burke, an eighteenth-century MP. He strongly argued that electors should entrust their MP with acting in their best interests. He phrased it as: 'Your representative owes you, not his industry only, but his judgement; and he betrays, instead of serving you, if he sacrifices it to your opinion.'

The MP is trusted by their voters to do what they consider is in their constituents' best interests, listening to their views but not being bound by them. It involves exercising their own judgement. An MP voting according to their own conscience, for example over abortion or euthanasia, would be reflecting this model.

The delegate model

REVISED

This is the opposite of the trustee model. MPs are viewed as mouthpieces for their constituents and entirely bound by their wishes. An MP voting against a planning or transport decision that is very unpopular in their constituency would be reflecting this model.

Zac Goldsmith stood down as a Conservative MP and resigned his Richmond Park seat in 2016 to fulfil a promise made to his voters about opposing a third runway for Heathrow. He stood as an independent at the ensuing by-election but was defeated, suggesting that voters may not always respect adherence by MPs to the delegate model.

Mandate theory

REVISED

MPs are elected primarily to carry out the manifesto promises of their party. This is the prevalent model in modern British politics, given the power and discipline of political parties. It reflects the fact that most votes an MP receives are because of party allegiance, not their own personality.

The role and influence of MPs and peers

What role do MPs and peers have?

REVISED

Both MPs and peers may:
- vote on legislation
- sit on parliamentary committees
- serve in the government as a minister or on the opposition frontbench (shadow cabinet)
- contribute to debates and ask questions of ministers
- introduce their own bills (private members' bills) to parliament
- make media appearances and give interviews
- enjoy parliamentary privilege

In addition, MPs have the following roles:
- Undertaking constituency casework: MPs have a duty to serve all their constituents, not merely those who voted for them.

- Holding regular surgeries: most MPs hold regular surgeries where the public can meet them and raise issues directly with them. This may be **lobbying** on a particular issue such as a hospital closure or to discuss personal matters such as those relating to housing or immigration. This could be seen as an example of parliament fulfilling its traditional role of **redress of grievances**. MPs employ constituency caseworkers to handle much of this work.
- Undertaking backbench rebellions: MPs from the governing party have increasingly been willing to vote against their own government. Recent notable rebellions occurred over air strikes in Syria in 2013 and aspects of the Brexit bill. Backbench rebellions are especially effective when a government has a small overall majority, such as the Cameron/May government (2015–17).
- Having a key initial role in the selection of party leader: both Labour and the Conservatives require leadership candidates to secure a set number of nominations from their sitting MPs before a vote of the wider party membership.
- Providing **democratic legitimacy** to government.

In addition, peers have the following roles:

- Contributing specialised insights in debates: peers often come from a wider range of backgrounds such as science, the arts, business and academia than members of the House of Commons so are able to contribute more specialised insights in debates.
- Maintaining independence: many peers are independent (**crossbenchers**) so are less likely to be swayed by party-political considerations.
- Revising and advising on legislation: the Lords as a whole has a key role in revising and advising on legislation. It is often known as the 'think again' house. Given its lack of any democratic **mandate** (and the Parliament Act), it cannot block legislation or force its views on government or the Commons.

Lobbying Attempting to influence the actions, policies or decisions of MPs.

Redress of grievances The right of citizens to get wrongs or injustices put right. In this example, a constituent might try to get their MP to put pressure on a government department or local council to treat a complaint more fairly. An MP could also do this by asking a parliamentary question or possibly by attempting to bring in a private members' bill to address the issue.

Democratic legitimacy The authority a body (here, the Commons) possesses if it is elected and accountable to the people via free and fair elections.

Crossbenchers Non-party-political peers. In effect, they are independent members of the Lords; an example is the former top civil servant Lord Kerslake.

Mandate The authority, given by the electorate, to carry out a policy. A party that wins a large majority of seats in the general election can be said to have a strong mandate from the people.

The Lords and representation

REVISED

As an unelected chamber, the Lords does not represent voters directly. Many of its members are affiliated to a political party, often being retired or defeated MPs (e.g. Lord Prescott was previously deputy prime minister), so they indirectly fulfil the mandate representation model.

Some peers are chosen on account of their distinction and achievements, in particular spheres of public life such as sport or the arts (e.g. the Paralympian and broadcaster Tanni Grey-Thompson), so, again, indirectly they represent those interests.

Exam practice answers and quick quizzes at **www.hoddereducation.co.uk/myrevisionnotesdownloads**

The significance of the Commons and the Lords

The work of committees

The work of the various committees is summarised in Table 2.3.

Table 2.3 Committees and their functions, characteristics and significance

Type of committee	Key functions and characteristics	Significance
Public bill committees	• Go through bills clause by clause, debate and suggest amendments. • Temporary, only meet while a bill is in the committee stage of the legislative process.	• Ensure bills are properly written and can fulfil the aims of their writers. • An opportunity for other MPs, peers and interest groups to lobby and suggest changes. • Major changes are unlikely as the governing party has a majority on the committee and **party whips** choose the members on each committee.
Commons select committees	• Provide a more general oversight of the workings of government departments and ministerial actions. • Less party political and partisan, for example sit in a horseshoe form rather than as two opposing sides facing each other. Aim for greater cross-party collaboration and consensus. • Many are chaired by opposition backbenchers. • Able to select their own areas for investigation and can summon witnesses.	• Comprised entirely of backbench MPs. • Committee chairs are elected by their fellow MPs, not selected by party whips. • Produce reports to which the government must usually reply within 60 days. • The government is not obliged to carry out any findings or recommendations in their reports. • Their reports and hearings often generate publicity in the media.
Lords select committees	• Investigate specialist subjects, taking advantage of the Lords' expertise and the greater amount of time (compared to MPs) available to them to examine issues. • Currently six main committees covering: the EU, communications, science and technology, economic affairs, the constitution and international relations.	• Often contain genuine specialists in their field, e.g. Lord Norton of Louth, Constitution Committee and a leading academic in constitutional and political affairs. • The governing party does not have a majority on the committees.
Public Accounts Committee (Commons only)	• Traditionally chaired by an experienced opposition backbencher (Meg Hillier in 2018). • Scrutinises value for money in public spending and how well/efficiently the government delivers public services.	• Covers a wide range of policy areas. Recent reports have ranged from unauthorised redundancy payments associated with High Speed 2 to the cost of NHS clinical negligence.
Backbench Business Committee (Commons only)	• Selects topics for debate in parliament on days not given over to government business. Such debates can take place both in the chamber and in Westminster Hall. • Oversees e-petitions.	• Enables backbenchers to have a greater say in what is debated. • Topics have included the conflict in Yemen and Jobcentre Plus office closures. • Such debates are better at raising issues than generating legislation or government action.

→

Type of committee	Key functions and characteristics	Significance
Commons Liaison Committee	• Comprises all the chairs of the Commons select committees. • Usually chaired by a senior and independent-minded backbencher of the governing party (Dr Sarah Wollaston in 2018). • Chooses select committee reports for debate in Westminster Hall. • Questions the prime minister on aspects of public policy, usually three times a year.	• Provides a more measured and focused way for ordinary MPs to make the prime minister accountable, without the theatricals of PMQs. • Coordinates the roles of select committees. • Has no ability to force the government or prime minister to change policy.

How effective and significant are select committees?

Between 1997 and 2010 select committees produced around 1,500 inquiry reports (or 110 a year) and almost 40,000 recommendations. High-profile reports have included those on phone-hacking by *News International* and the working practices of Sports Direct.

It is estimated that around 40% of committee recommendations are accepted by the government and a similar proportion go on to be implemented. Around one-third of recommendations for major policy changes succeed. The 2016 report by the Work and Pensions Select Committee into the collapse of BHS and the loss of much of the employees' pension fund resulted in the company and its owners being reported to the Pensions Regulator.

Committee chairs are paid a salary equivalent to that of a junior minister, offering MPs an attractive career alternative to ministerial office.

> **Party whips** MPs in charge of persuading their party's MPs to remain loyal. They seek to do this by argument and sometimes inducements such as the prospect of promotion. The government chief whip in 2018 was Julian Smith.

Role of the opposition

REVISED

The opposition's role is to:
- provide scrutiny and reasoned criticism of government policies and actions in debates and via parliamentary questions
- suggest amendments to bills
- argue for alternatives — what they would do if in power
- provide a 'government in waiting', especially with a shadow cabinet
- nominate the topics for debates on 20 days in each parliamentary session; 17 go to the official opposition party, 3 to the second largest opposition party

> **Revision activity**
>
> Make a list of five current prominent cabinet members and write down the corresponding member of the shadow cabinet.

Influence of parliament on government decisions

REVISED

Parliament influences government decisions in the following ways:
- the committee system and committee reports
- election of select committee chairs (no longer appointed by party whips)
- debates and questions
- backbench rebellions in the Commons
- informal lobbying of ministers by MPs and peers
- amending legislation, especially in the Lords

However, there are limits to parliament's influence on government:
- Governments can ignore select committee reports.
- Select committees are poorly resourced compared to government departments.

Exam practice answers and quick quizzes at **www.hoddereducation.co.uk/myrevisionnotesdownloads**

- Government majorities usually see off backbench revolts.
- Party whips ensure party discipline.
- The government is in control of most of the parliamentary timetable.
- Many MPs aspire to promotion so are wary of upsetting the party leadership.
- The government can use its Commons majority to override Lords' amendments or rejection of a bill, using if necessary the Parliament Act.

Party discipline in the Commons

REVISED

Both the governing and opposition parties use a whipping system to enforce party discipline and minimise internal dissent in parliamentary votes.

Most governments have large and stable enough majorities to defeat backbench rebellions (e.g. the Blair government and student tuition fees) and thus outvote the opposition. Party discipline is most fragile when a government has only a small or non-existent majority and seeks to get through legislation that is controversial with some of its own backbenchers and the main opposition parties. However, much of the time party discipline does not need to be enforced as MPs will naturally vote the way their leadership wants.

The most important votes are termed **three-line whips**, when MPs must turn up and vote the way their leaders wish. Votes on matters of conscience such as assisted dying or abortion are not usually whipped, allowing MPs a **free vote**.

Whips exert further control over party discipline by partly controlling the allocation of MPs to both select and public bill committees, although select committee chairs are now elected by a secret ballot of all MPs, thereby weakening the whips' power.

> **Three-line whips** Parliamentary votes when MPs must follow the voting orders of the whips. Failure to do so by a minister would lead to resignation or dismissal. Backbenchers who frequently rebel are unlikely to be offered posts in the government or on the opposition front bench.
>
> **Free vote** A vote when MPs are free to vote how they wish, rather than being instructed to vote a certain way by the party leadership.

Government control of civil servants

Traditionally, the government had a lot of control over civil servants appearing before select committees. The original **Osmotherly Rules** allowed plenty of scope for senior civil servants to be evasive and vague in their answers before committees. However, they have recently been revised and civil servants are now required to be as helpful as possible in providing accurate, truthful and full information in accordance with the duties and responsibilities of the Civil Service Code. For example, in 2016 the Home Affairs Select Committee ejected Oliver Robbins, a senior civil servant, for failing to respond adequately to questions about the budget of the UK's border force. Civil servants must balance their answers with due regard to ministerial accountability and not deliberately undermine their political masters — the ministers.

> **Osmotherly Rules** Guidance given to civil servants and other government officials appearing before select committees. Various versions of the rules have been in operation since 1980, but they have never been formally accepted by parliament. The rules were most recently updated in October 2014.

How parliament interacts with other branches of government

Key points

REVISED

- Parliament provides the personnel for government: prime minister and ministers.
- It is the forum where government is primarily called to account and scrutinised.

- It passes the laws that are then interpreted and enforced by the judiciary.
- Any laws passed must be compatible with international agreements such as the European Convention on Human Rights (ECHR) and (until Brexit) EU law.

Summary

You should now have an understanding of:
- the key features of parliament
- how parliament checks the executive
- the main stages of the legislative process
- the different theories of representation
- the powers and importance of MPs and peers
- how MPs and peers can influence governments
- how committees function in parliament
- the extent to which parliament as a body can influence government decisions
- how party discipline is enforced
- how parliament relates to other branches of government

Exam practice

AS

1 Explain, with examples, what the difference is between a select committee and a public bill committee. [6]
2 'Parliament provides few opportunities for backbench MPs to influence the government of the day.' Analyse and evaluate this statement. [25]

A-level

3 Explain and analyse three stages in the parliamentary legislative process. [9]

Read the following extract.

Although there are three basic theories of representation, in modern-day Britain the mandate model is clearly the most important. Most voters make their choice on the basis of party alone. The character and abilities of an individual MP count for virtually nothing when it comes to voting patterns. The party manifesto and the quality of each party's leader are really what are up for election and judgement every 5 years. Few MPs would ever consider themselves as bound by the wishes of the local electorate beyond the narrow sense of party loyalty.

Yet there are occasions when MPs do act as trustees and exercise their own judgements. The growing number of backbench rebellions is evidence of this. The same also applies to free votes in the Commons that involve matters of conscience or religious belief such as that on same-sex marriage. In 2013, 136 Conservative MPs voted against the measure despite it being backed by then leader and prime minister David Cameron. Votes on euthanasia and the Human Fertilisation and Embryology Bill offer other occasions when MPs have been free of the party whip. In these cases, we can clearly see that the Burkean theory of representation is well and truly alive. MPs have conflicting loyalties to balance but, in the end, the need to be faithful to their party's manifesto pledges remains the most important. Few would wish to be deselected by their local party and then lose a subsequent election standing as an independent.

Source: Original material, 2018

4 Analyse, evaluate and compare the arguments in the above extract for and against the view that MPs act primarily as trustees when it comes to representation. [25]

Answers and quick quiz 2 online

ONLINE

3 The prime minister and cabinet

Key points

- The prime minister and their cabinet constitute the government or executive of the UK. They are the main source of policy making and parliamentary legislation.
- Although prime ministers enjoy considerable freedom such as their ability to choose ministers, they can also be vulnerable, especially if they only have a small Commons majority or are faring badly in the polls.
- All members of the government (and especially the cabinet) must, in public at least, display loyalty to the prime minister and defend all aspects of government policy.
- Many of the powers of the prime minister tend to be variable, not least according to the prevailing political climate.

The prime minister

Main functions and role

The prime minister is the head of the executive (government), chair of the cabinet and in charge of the civil service. The role includes:

- leading the government, with overall responsibility for both domestic and foreign policy
- selecting the cabinet and all junior government posts
- being the dominant figure in the **core executive**
- representing the country abroad and attending international functions of world leaders, e.g. G7 summits
- being the party leader
- being the main 'defender and explainer' of government policy and actions in both parliament and the media
- chairing cabinet meetings
- heading up the civil service
- being the monarch's first minister and *primus inter pares* with other ministers

> **Core executive** The collective term for the key players in government policy making. It comprises the prime minister, the cabinet and its various committees, the Cabinet Office and senior civil servants.
>
> *Primus inter pares* The traditional notion that the prime minister is merely the 'first among equals' among fellow members of the cabinet. In reality, modern prime ministers have far more power.

> **Exam tip**
>
> Be careful to distinguish between the terms 'executive' (prime minister and cabinet) and 'core executive' (prime minister, cabinet, its various committees, Cabinet Office and senior civil servants). The core executive is a more wide-ranging term and usefully suggests how power is spread beyond just the immediate circle of ministers and prime minister.

Main powers and resources

The prime minister's main powers and resources include:

- prerogative powers (the royal prerogative)
- shaping and deciding national policy
- de facto commander-in-chief of the armed forces

- patronage — choosing their cabinet and promoting, demoting and reshuffling members as appropriate
- arranging the structure of cabinet committees and often chairing many committees
- high media profile — plenty of opportunities to explain and defend government actions to the public and to parliament
- as leader of the largest party in the Commons, they are normally able to command a working majority to get through their legislative plans, which gives them a lot of control over parliamentary business
- able to make use of the civil service (especially the Cabinet Office) and special advisers (SpAds) for policy input and advice
- usually able to claim authority or a mandate from the people by winning the general election. Prime ministers who assume office mid-term, such as Gordon Brown in 2007, are often said to be weakened by the lack of a direct mandate

The cabinet

Key points

REVISED

The cabinet is the team of around 23 senior government ministers and other key officials such as the chief whip, who are directly appointed by the prime minister. They normally meet once a week on Thursday mornings. It is chaired by the prime minister, who also largely determines the agenda. Much of its detailed work is done in cabinet committees. Most members are MPs, although there are normally a couple of peers present as well including the leader of the House of Lords.

Prime ministers often **reshuffle** the cabinet in order to bring in new talent or 'freshen up' their team, to sack under-performing ministers or to fill gaps caused by death or resignation. Theresa May undertook a cabinet reshuffle in July 2018. For example, Jeremy Hunt moved from health secretary to foreign secretary.

The cabinet's proceedings are kept secret and all members publicly support its decisions. This principle is known as **collective cabinet responsibility**. Different prime ministers have managed the cabinet in different ways, reflecting their own style and personality.

The cabinet is seen as the traditional basis for policy making in the UK. However, many have argued that, in reality, prime ministers rather than the cabinet as a whole dominate decision making, hence Lord Hailsham's famous 1976 reference to an 'elective dictatorship'.

Formal votes on policy and decisions are rare; prime ministers usually aim for agreement by consensus. However, it was reported that in May 2018 the Brexit 'war cabinet' sub-committee rejected the prime minister's plan for a customs partnership with the EU by a vote of 6 to 5 against.

Reshuffle When ministers are moved around government departments; some will be promoted, some moved sideways and some sacked from government altogether. The most infamous reshuffle was carried out by Harold Macmillan in 1962 when he sacked seven cabinet colleagues, an event known as the 'Night of the Long Knives'.

Collective cabinet responsibility The principle whereby all members of the cabinet support its decisions in public, even if they disagree with them in private and argued against them in cabinet discussion. It is seen as vital to the effective functioning of cabinet government.

The cabinet is sometimes characterised by informal smaller groupings such as the **inner cabinet** (or 'kitchen cabinet') comprising just a handful of senior cabinet ministers. Some prime ministers, such as Tony Blair, preferred even smaller meetings, known as 'sofa government', often with individual ministers. These are sometimes regarded as undermining proper cabinet government.

> **Inner cabinet** A smaller, more informal group of senior ministers who meet outside of regular sessions of the full cabinet. It is often seen as the place where the real decisions are made.

Cabinet committees

- Cabinet committees are groups of ministers that take collective decisions, many of them routine. They can also include sub-committees.
- The composition, membership and terms of reference are decided solely by the prime minister.
- They tend to comprise ministers from several related departments to enable **joined-up government**, e.g. the Social Reform Committee includes the secretaries of state for education, health and social care as well as work and pensions.
- Their decisions are as binding on the rest of the cabinet as those made by the full cabinet.
- There was a significant reduction to five main committees in 2017, with four out of them chaired by the prime minister.

> **Joined-up government** A policy to make different departments in the same government work together.

Some examples of cabinet committees are given in Table 3.1.

Table 3.1 Examples of cabinet committees in 2018

Committee	Functions/remit
National Security Council	The main forum for discussion and consideration of government objectives for national security. Looks strategically at the issue. Not the same as the emergency council known as Cobra
European Union Exit and Trade Committee	Oversees the UK's exit negotiations with the EU
Social Reform Committee	Oversees and agrees social policy reforms, e.g. the introduction of universal credit and ways to improve social mobility

How policy is made

Key players

REVISED

All the key players listed in Table 3.2 play a role in policy making. Different policies will involve the key players to a varying extent.

Table 3.2 Key players in the policy-making process

Key player	Examples in practice	Significance
Prime minister	• Most prime ministers enter No 10 with a clear policy agenda often based on personal convictions and principles, e.g. Tony Blair and constitutional change. • These often have a catchy strap line such as David Cameron's 'Big Society'.	• Very important. Prime ministers seek to prioritise their key policies so as to make their mark and leave behind a tangible legacy. • A working majority in the Commons means they can normally ensure such legislation gets through, although prime ministers with small or non-existent majorities have a harder time. Those in coalition government have to negotiate policy with the junior coalition party.

→

Key player	Examples in practice	Significance
The cabinet	● Will normally discuss and debate policy initiatives and 'rubber stamp' them. ● Where there are disagreements such as over spending priorities, these are often resolved at cabinet meetings.	● Often considerable, especially if the party is divided, a policy is controversial and/or the prime minister is seen as relatively weak. ● Much of the finer detail for the Brexit negotiations from 2017 onwards was thrashed out in the cabinet.
Senior civil servants	● Can offer advice and guidance to government ministers. Crucial in the actual delivery of policy, e.g. the 2012 London Olympics and the National Citizen Service. ● Influence ministers by 'speaking truth unto power'. ● Until late 2018, the head of the Civil Service and cabinet secretary was Sir Jeremy Heywood.	● As permanent and non-party political, their advice should be unbiased and objective. ● Should not offer advice about the rights or wrongs of a particular policy but advise on implementation, legality, cost implications and other practicalities. ● Provide long experience of government and handling different issues and policies across the political spectrum. ● Increasingly share responsibility for providing policy advice with special advisers.
Special advisers (SpAds)	● Party-political figures hand-picked by the prime minister. ● Temporary civil servants; unlike permanent civil servants, not required to offer balanced advice. ● Normally replaced by an incoming prime minister, even one from the same party. ● 88 special advisers in post in December 2017 (compared to 423,000 civil servants in total).	● Have assumed increasing prominence and notoriety in recent years, e.g. Alastair Campbell (Tony Blair) and Nick Timothy (Theresa May). ● Frequently seen to 'have the ear of the prime minister' and to have played a major part in policy formation, e.g. Theresa May's original policy pledge to reintroduce some grammar schools. ● Special advisers often come up with the 'big vision' initiatives. Prime minister David Cameron's 'Big Society' was largely the idea of his strategy guru and special adviser, Steve Hilton.

Manifesto pledges

REVISED

Manifesto pledges are perhaps the easiest to decide upon as the party in power will have agreed these already, although a minority/coalition government will have to make a deal with other parties. For example, after the inconclusive 2017 election, prime minister Theresa May struck a deal with the Democratic Unionist Party (DUP), promising additional funding for Northern Ireland and keeping a pledge to increase state pensions by at least 2.5% a year. The DUP is the largest political party in Northern Ireland with 10 MPs. It is strongly in favour of keeping Northern Ireland within the UK, as well as being pro–Brexit and socially conservative (e.g. anti–abortion).

> **Exam tip**
>
> The DUP are not in a formal coalition with the Conservatives as the Liberal Democrats were between 2010 and 2015. They therefore have no ministers in government and only agree to support the government in crucial votes of confidence (to prevent a no confidence vote in the Commons from ending the government) and supply (it supplies the government with funds by passing the government budget), in return for key policy concessions. The formal name for this arrangement is a confidence and supply deal.

Collaboration

Many policy decisions and strategies require consultation and cooperation between different ministers and government departments (e.g. Brexit). Although the prime minister has the final say on policy, in effect they are often constrained by political reality such as backbench rebellions and the threat of ministerial resignations. Prime ministers who are not very collaborative in policy making such as Margaret Thatcher and Tony Blair can find themselves dangerously isolated and vulnerable.

Some policy is the result of unforeseen events or emergencies. This applies, for example, to responses (and restrictions) following terrorist attacks such as the 7/7 London bombings.

The relationship between prime minister and cabinet

Key points

- In theory, the relationship should be harmonious and fruitful because:
  - ○ the cabinet is selected purely by the prime minister and requires no approval from parliament (unlike in the USA where Senate ratification is required)
  - ○ the prime minister and the cabinet are (usually) from the same political party, coalition government being the exception
- In reality, however, most prime ministers experience fractious relations with the cabinet some of the time due to a number of factors:
  - ○ Political parties are broad-based so contain a variety of views and therefore factions emerge, such as **Brexiteers** and **Remainers** under Theresa May. Prime ministers need to include all the main strands of party opinion in their cabinet to keep their party relatively united.
  - ○ Most cabinets contain 'big beasts', politicians who are too senior or popular to leave out, e.g. Boris Johnson in Theresa May's cabinet until he resigned of his own accord in July 2018 over the prime minister's Brexit deal proposals.
  - ○ As cabinets contain some of the brightest and best MPs, they also include many individuals with ambitions and/or high egos. Any cabinet contains a mixture of foes, rivals and allies.
  - ○ Factions often gather around strong individuals, e.g. **Blairites** and **Brownites**.
  - ○ Each minister is lobbying for departmental resources and wants priority given to their department's financial demands, whether it is more money for the NHS or the latest military equipment.

> **Brexiteers** Those who supported the Leave campaign in the 2016 EU referendum.
>
> **Remainers** Those who supported the Remain campaign in the 2016 EU referendum.
>
> **Blairites** Labour MPs regarded as being loyal to prime minister Tony Blair during the Labour governments of 1997–2010. Peter Mandelson was a prominent member of this group.
>
> **Brownites** Labour MPs regarded as being loyal to chancellor Gordon Brown during the Labour governments of 1997–2010. Ed Balls was a prominent member of this group.

The difference between individual and collective responsibility

Individual (ministerial) responsibility

- The notion that each minister is personally responsible for the actions and outcomes in their department.
- Involves answering questions in the Commons and in the media on behalf of their department.

- In theory, mistakes and policy failures in a department could lead to a minister resigning. In practice, this is rare and ministers tend to resign for other reasons.
- Less significant nowadays as ministers often devolve blame for policy failures to civil servants or heads of executive agencies. For example, in 2013 Iain Duncan Smith blamed civil servants for IT failings following a scathing **National Audit Office (NAO)** report on the introduction of universal credit.
- Ministers whose personal conduct falls below that expected of someone in public life and/or breaches the Ministerial Code would be expected to resign or face dismissal by the prime minister. This is often linked to personal scandal. The Ministerial Code was first issued in 2010 and its key principles include:
  - ○ avoiding any conflict of interest between private interests and public duties
  - ○ not accepting any gifts or offers of hospitality that could be construed as bribery or attempting to influence decisions
  - ○ upholding the principle of civil service impartiality
  - ○ abiding by the principles of collective cabinet responsibility
  - ○ not meeting foreign dignitaries or politicians without the prime minister's permission and without civil servants present

> **National Audit Office (NAO)**
> An independent government body responsible for scrutinising the use of public money and ensuring it is spent efficiently and appropriately. It is essentially the government's spending watchdog.

Case study: Dismissal for breaching the Ministerial Code

Priti Patel was the international development secretary who was sacked by Theresa May in November 2017 for not being open and honest about secret meetings with Israeli ministers and businesspeople while on a private holiday in Israel.	Not only did Priti Patel break the Ministerial Code by meeting senior Israeli officials without the knowledge of the prime minister and the Foreign Office, it also emerged that she had been less than completely truthful with Theresa May when the story first appeared.

Collective cabinet responsibility

REVISED

- The convention that all ministers, and not just those in the cabinet, are bound by government policies and must defend and promote them in public.
- A minister who cannot in good conscience agree with government policy should resign.
- Occasionally, collective cabinet responsibility is suspended by the prime minister when there are clear and open divisions within the cabinet. This is principally true of EU membership. Both Harold Wilson (Labour prime minister 1964–70 and 1974–76) and David Cameron formally suspended it before referendums on continued membership of the EEC/EU.
- Free votes, such as those on issues of conscience, are also not normally bound by the convention.
- Occasionally, ministers can publicly breach collective cabinet responsibility and survive. For example, Ken Clarke and Theresa May made conflicting statements about the future of the Human Rights Act in 2010–11.
- Some ministers secretly breach collective cabinet responsibility by speaking to journalists **'off the record'** or by leaking documents to the press.
- In January 2018, Boris Johnson was criticised for revealing in advance that he would argue at cabinet for £5 billion extra to be spent on the NHS.

> **'Off the record'** When a minister or other politician speaks to a journalist on the condition of complete anonymity. Therefore, a story will refer vaguely to 'sources close to the prime minister' and not mention a name.

- It enables the prime minister and government to present a strong and united front to the media, the public and their backbenchers.

Now test yourself

1 How often does the cabinet normally meet?
2 Who appoints, removes and reshuffles the cabinet?
3 How many full cabinet committees were there in 2018 under Theresa May?
4 When was the Ministerial Code first introduced?
5 Which prime minister suspended collective cabinet responsibility over continued membership of the European Economic Community (EEC)?
6 Name one minister who breached collective cabinet responsibility but survived.
7 Which cabinet minister had to resign because they met members of a foreign government without civil servants present on a private trip abroad?
8 What was the major divide within Theresa May's cabinet after the 2017 election?
9 Who do ministers often blame for operational failures in their departments?
10 What does *primus inter pares* mean?

Answers on p. 109

Resignations

REVISED

Table 3.3 outlines two resignations owing to individual and collective cabinet responsibility.

Table 3.3 **Examples of resignations**

Example	Cause of resignation	Details and background
Sir Thomas Dugdale's 1954 resignation as Minister of Agriculture	Individual (ministerial) responsibility	• An official inquiry found serious flaws in procedures and practices by civil servants regarding a case of compulsory purchase of farmland for a military airfield. • Dugdale resigned although he had nothing to do with the original decisions. • He resigned because he accepted full responsibility for the actions of officials in his department.
Iain Duncan Smith's 2016 resignation as work and pensions secretary	Collective cabinet responsibility	• Duncan Smith left David Cameron's cabinet over planned cuts to disability benefits, which he described as a 'compromise too far'. • He felt unable on principle to support such a policy. • Other examples of ministerial resignations over policy difference include Robin Cook in 2003 over the Iraq War and Greg Hands in 2018 over the proposed third runway at Heathrow.

Why else do ministers resign or lose office?

- Removed via a cabinet reshuffle to make way for fresh faces.
- Seen as under-performing, for example being a poor media or Commons performer.
- Ill health: James Brokenshire resigned from the cabinet as Northern Ireland secretary to undergo cancer treatment in January 2018. A subsequent cabinet reshuffle following Amber Rudd's resignation (due to the Windrush scandal) in April enabled him to return to the cabinet later in 2018.
- Personal scandal: easily the most common cause. This usually involves financial misconduct (such as expenses, e.g. Maria Miller as culture secretary in 2014) or sexual misconduct (such as Michael Fallon as defence secretary in 2017). In such cases, the tipping point is normally when they lose the prime minister's confidence and become a distraction to the overall work of the government.

Revision activity

Research and make bullet point notes on the following:
- three ministers since 2010 who have resigned due to personal scandal
- three ministers since 2010 who been removed in cabinet reshuffles
- three ministers since 2010 who have been promoted in cabinet reshuffles

Include the name, date, post and a brief explanation.

Typical mistake

Don't include policy failure as a common cause of ministerial resignation. Most major policy initiatives are decided by the whole cabinet and the prime minister. Policy implementation is also not a frequent cause nowadays for resignation. Ministers are much more willing to blame senior civil servants or executive agency chiefs when things go wrong.

Now test yourself

TESTED

11 Read the scenarios below and decide which category of resignation is correct, selecting from:
  (a) individual ministerial responsibility
  (b) collective cabinet responsibility
  (c) loss of confidence by the prime minister
  (d) personal scandal

Scenario	Category
A tabloid newspaper reports on a minister persuading his wife to lie to the police so he avoids getting speeding points on his driving licence	
A minister resigns because of swingeing cuts to their departmental budget	
The prime minister is facing mounting calls from the media and even some backbench MPs to sack a minister who is alleged to have made anti-Semitic remarks at a private dinner	
A minister resigns after their department is heavily criticised for failing to handle asylum requests quickly and fairly	

Answers on p. 109

The power to determine policy making

Introduction of the poll tax, 1990

REVISED

Background/motives

- A longstanding Conservative policy to reform local government taxation and end domestic rates, and a 1987 manifesto pledge.
- Many Conservatives wanted to rein in high-spending Labour councils, many of whose voters did not pay rates.
- A desire to spread the cost of local government services such as education and social care more fairly. Domestic rates taxed homes regardless of the number of residents (and their use of local services) or their income. They also were not directly payable by tenants.
- The poll tax (the official name was the community charge) was a flat rate tax payable by nearly all adults.
- The policy was strongly supported by Margaret Thatcher herself. She personally annotated many of the briefings and memorandums about the proposals.
- First trialled in Scotland where it had proved unpopular and difficult to implement.
- Thatcher, although undefeated after three general elections and with a decent Commons majority, was facing increasing criticism of her dictatorial style and unwillingness to listen to critics within her own party and even the cabinet.

Outcome

- Aroused strong hostility on the left; many refused to pay the new tax.
- Mass protests including a number of violent tax riots involving tens of thousands of protestors.
- Opposition was especially strong in staunchly Labour areas such as South Yorkshire, already alienated by the 1984–85 miners' strike and pit closures.
- Many of Thatcher's MPs disliked the policy and criticised the prime minister. The growing opposition from Tory MPs and supporters played a major part in a formal leadership challenge from ex-minister Michael Heseltine in November 1990. She failed to secure enough votes in the first ballot and subsequently resigned as prime minister and Tory leader soon afterwards.
- The policy was scrapped soon after Thatcher's resignation and replaced by the council tax.

Invasion of Iraq, 2003

REVISED

Background/motives

- In 1991 a UN-backed force including the UK had fought and defeated Iraq after it invaded Kuwait (Operation Desert Storm). This First Gulf War did not, however, remove Iraq's dictator, Saddam Hussein, from power.
- By 2003, the USA under President George W. Bush believed Saddam Hussein had a store of chemical or nuclear weapons (weapons of mass destruction or WMDs), which Saddam was on the verge of using.
- Bush persuaded his strong ally, prime minister Tony Blair, to support a pre-emptive invasion of Iraq to destroy the WMDs and remove Saddam Hussein.
- Blair secured the support of the Commons to go to war alongside the USA, by a vote of 412 to 149 in March 2003.
- Around 25% of Labour MPs rebelled against their own leadership, although only one cabinet minister (Robin Cook) resigned before the vote.
- Blair enjoyed a large Commons majority having won two elections, although he was facing increasing criticism from the left of his party for policies such as the introduction in 1998 of university tuition fees.

Outcome

- Although the conventional war was successful and Saddam Hussein was removed from power, Iraq itself descended into chaos and civil war. British and American troops had to stay on in Iraq for several more years.
- The war and the legacy conflict cost the lives of around 180 British troops and cost billions of pounds.
- There were huge anti-war protests across Britain and many consider the war to have been a major blemish on Blair's record as prime minister and to have hastened his resignation in 2007.
- There was increasing pressure for Britain to withdraw its troops from Iraq, although the last British forces only left in 2011.
- The Iraq invasion, along with British involvement in Afghanistan, has made subsequent British governments much more wary of committing troops overseas in major combat roles.
- It was subsequently revealed that the threat from Saddam's WMDs was much exaggerated.

Comparing these events

Table 3.4 highlights some of the similarities and differences between Thatcher's introduction of the poll tax and Blair's invasion of Iraq.

Table 3.4 Similarities and differences between these events

Similarities	Differences
<ul><li>Both were very damaging to the prime minister of the time and seen as major blots on their reputations.</li><li>There was a strong personal commitment to the policy by the prime minister.</li><li>Seen as examples of the prime minister dictating policy largely alone and not taking criticism seriously or listening to advice that did not accord with their own views.</li><li>Occurred under prime ministers who were already well established in office: Thatcher 11 years and Blair 6 years.</li><li>Aroused strong criticism within their own parties.</li><li>Both were formally voted upon and approved by parliament.</li><li>Many public protests which were often violent.</li><li>In each case the policy was reversed/wound down by their successors.</li></ul>	<ul><li>The poll tax was opposed by Labour, whereas most Conservatives backed Blair over the invasion of Iraq.</li><li>Thatcher resigned soon after the poll tax was introduced, whereas Blair remained prime minister for several more years.</li><li>One was domestic policy and a manifesto pledge, whereas the other was about foreign policy and a response to events/pressure from the USA.</li><li>The invasion of Iraq was arguably a more damaging policy given the loss of life and financial cost.</li></ul>

Revision activity

Create a list of pros and cons to explain why an MP might rebel against their party leadership.

Relations between government and parliament

Theory

The government should be checked by and answerable to parliament. Ministers should be personally accountable to parliament, e.g. via oral questions. Governments should easily be able to get their business through Westminster due to a working majority, the power of the party whips and the limited power of the Lords.

Reality

Governments often avoid effective scrutiny in the main chamber due to party loyalties and the theatrical or ritualistic nature of questions, especially Prime Minister's Questions. The most effective scrutiny of government arguably comes via select committees or bodies such as the National Audit Office (NAO). The NAO, for example, produced a report in 2018 highlighting a £2.9 billion shortfall in the programme to renew the Trident nuclear submarine fleet.

Ministers rarely take personal responsibility for failings in their departments. Ministers most commonly resign due to personal scandals rather than policy differences (inability to accept collective cabinet responsibility) or ministerial accountability.

The growing willingness of backbenchers to rebel means that government policies do not always have a smooth ride through the Commons. This is especially true if their majority is small or the prime minister is already facing a high level of criticism from within their own party.

Summary

You should now have an understanding of:
- the key powers of the prime minister
- the composition and function of the cabinet
- the role and importance of cabinet committees
- how government policy is made
- the importance of the prime minister in policy making (via two case studies, one before 1997 and one after)
- the difference between individual and collective responsibility
- reasons why ministers might resign
- the relationship between government and parliament

Exam practice

AS

1 Explain, with examples, what the difference is between individual and collective cabinet responsibility. [6]
2 'The modern prime minister is much more than *primus inter pares*.' Analyse and evaluate this statement. [25]

A-level

3 Explain and analyse three key aspects of cabinet committees. [9]
4 'The personal involvement of the prime minister is the most dominant factor in the making of policy.' Analyse and evaluate this statement with reference to any two examples (one pre- and one post-1997) that you have studied. [25]

Answers and quick quiz 3 online

ONLINE

4 The judiciary

Key points

- The judiciary is concerned with applying the law and ensuring that government and other public institutions such as local councils follow their own rules.
- The judiciary also has a crucial role in protecting citizens' rights.
- The UK judiciary is organised hierarchically.
- The UK does not have a unified legal system and there are differences between England and Wales, and Scotland and Northern Ireland.
- The **UK Supreme Court (UKSC)** is the only judicial institution that has authority in all parts of the UK.

> **UK Supreme Court (UKSC)**
> The highest court of appeal in the UK. It has the power to make judgements based on EU law and the European Convention on Human Rights (ECHR).

Organisation and key principles

Organisation

The judiciary in England and Wales forms a strict hierarchy of importance (Figure 4.1). For example, judges of the Court of Appeal are generally given more weight than district judges sitting in county courts and magistrates' courts.

> **Exam tip**
>
> There is no need to learn the functions of all the different courts, but you should be aware of the hierarchical nature of them and how each level can overrule those below them.

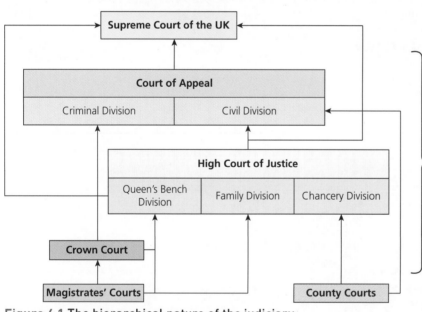

Figure 4.1 The hierarchical nature of the judiciary

Key principles

In order to understand the function and powers of the judiciary properly, you need to know some of the key ideas that underpin it.

Judicial independence and impartiality

Judicial independence is the notion that judges are free from government interference (i.e. they are independent). This is largely maintained via an independent appointments process and permanent job security for judges. Salaries are set by an independent body not the government.

Judicial impartiality or neutrality is the notion that judges are neutral/objective when it comes to making their judgements and not swayed by personal opinion or popular pressure. This is ensured by professional training and the requirements that UKSC judges must have considerable legal experience. However, the background of many judges is seen by some as unbalanced and thus harmful to true neutrality.

Separation of powers

The judiciary is separate, both physically and in terms of personnel, from parliament and the government. This is seen as crucial to judicial independence and upholding the rule of law.

Ultra vires

This means that everyone is subject to the law of the land, including the government. If governments or other public bodies are deemed by the courts to have exceeded their powers, their actions are declared *ultra vires*, i.e. beyond the power of the law and therefore illegal, and must be reversed. Such decisions are often made after the process of judicial review.

Judicial review

A judicial review is court proceedings where judges review the legality of a decision or action made by a public body including the government. Any challenge is to *the way* in which a decision has been made, i.e. about processes, not the rights and wrongs of the conclusion reached.

> **Typical mistake**
>
> Don't confuse a judicial review in the UK with the American process where courts can declare an action or law unconstitutional and 'strike it down'. No British courts have this power.

> **Typical mistake**
>
> Make sure you are clear about the difference between judicial independence and judicial impartiality/neutrality. Although similar, they are not the same thing.

Is the judiciary too powerful?

REVISED

Table 4.1 discusses whether the judiciary in the UK could be deemed to be too powerful.

Table 4.1 Is the judiciary in the UK too powerful?

Yes	No
• Judges, unlike MPs, are unelected and cannot be removed easily. • The Human Rights Act 1998 means judges get involved in politics and often clash with the government, undermining both parliamentary sovereignty and democracy. • Judges make decisions that can have a huge impact, including over life and death (e.g. cases involving assisted dying or switching off life-support machines). • Judicial review means that judges can end up forcing government departments and public bodies to change their policies.	• Judges need to be independent of politicians in order to be impartial and fair to everyone. • Judges only interpret laws passed by parliament. Parliament has chosen to sign up to the European Convention on Human Rights (ECHR) and to pass the Human Rights Act 1998, and could equally opt to reverse both actions. • Judges are very experienced legal professionals who are properly trained in looking at complex and difficult cases impartially. They are better suited than politicians who might be swayed by public opinion and the media. • The courts are there to make sure that those in power stick to the rules themselves. This is a necessary check to avoid arbitrary government. No one is above the law.

Composition and appointment of the judiciary

Appointment procedure

- Judges' appointments are based on merit and experience.
- Politicians have no real say in judicial appointments, unlike in the USA.
- Since 2006, all judges below the level of the Supreme Court have been appointed by the independent Judicial Appointments Commission (JAC) via an open and competitive application process. Before then, the **lord chancellor** had a role in the process. Nowadays, they have only a limited power of veto over JAC appointees.
- Many have criticised the UK judiciary regarding its composition in terms of gender, race and educational/social background. The judiciary, especially at the most senior levels, has been accused of being 'too privileged, pale and male'.

> **Lord chancellor** The government's senior minister in charge of the law and justice, and a political appointment. Until 2005, lord chancellors also acted as the head of the judiciary and as the speaker of the Lords. Today, those posts are held by others and the lord chancellor (David Gauke in 2018) is just a member of the cabinet and in charge of the Department of Justice.

Evidence of a lack of diversity among judges

- Under-representation of females: 25% in the UKSC in mid-2018 and 24% in the Court of Appeal in 2017.
- Lack of black, Asian and minority ethnic (BAME) judges: none in the UKSC in mid-2018 and 7% of all judges in 2017 (up from 6% in 2014).
- Fewer non-barristers, i.e. judges with a background as solicitors or legal executives: 34% of all judges in 2017, down from 37% in 2014.
- Domination of public school and Oxbridge background, especially among the top levels of the judiciary: 75% of the 12 UKSC justices serving in mid-2018 attended either Oxford or Cambridge.

> **Typical mistake**
>
> Remember that the judges for the Supreme Court are *not* appointed by the JAC but by a slightly different procedure (see p. 44).

Table 4.2 assesses whether a lack of diversity among the judiciary matters.

Table 4.2 Does a lack of diversity in the judiciary matter?

Yes	No
Judges do not reflect modern British society.	Unlike MPs, judges are not representatives of the people but are chosen for their professional expertise and on merit.
It could make it hard for judges to understand fully the cultural context of some cases.	Judges are not there to empathise but to apply the law neutrally and professionally.
There has been little improvement in judicial diversity in the last decade, such as in the UKSC.	Diversity is greater and growing lower down the judicial hierarchy. Changes at the top can only come about as the talent pool broadens lower down. It will alter eventually.
It reduces the public's trust in the judiciary and leads to biased 'pro-establishment' decisions.	The public would rather have judicial decisions in the hands of the best qualified. There is no evidence of an establishment bias. On the contrary, judges have often criticised governments and upheld the rights of minorities such as asylum seekers.
More input from democratically elected representatives in the appointments process would help bolster diversity.	This would almost inevitably lead to a dangerous politicisation of the judiciary.

The UK Supreme Court

Key points

REVISED

- Set up in 2009 following the Constitutional Reform Act 2005.
- Replaced the Law Lords as the highest court in the land.
- Physically and institutionally separate from parliament, therefore embodying the notion of the separation of powers.
- Comprises 12 judges.
- To be eligible for appointment, candidates must have served for either a minimum of 2 years in a senior judicial role or 15 years as a barrister or solicitor.
- Composition has been criticised for its lack of diversity (see p. 40), although its president in 2018 was Lady Hale.
- Judges enjoy permanent job security until reaching compulsory retirement age (70 in most cases). They cannot be removed by ministers or parliament unless for gross misconduct.
- Free of political pressure.

Main roles

REVISED

- The final court of appeal for all UK civil cases and criminal cases from England, Wales and Northern Ireland.
- Hears appeals on points of law from the general public and of national importance.
- Enforces the ECHR in the UK, which means it reduces the number of cases on behalf of UK citizens heard in the European Court of Human Rights (ECtHR) in Strasbourg.
- Acts as the final court of appeal for a number of British overseas territories and former colonies such as Jamaica.

UKSC and Europe

REVISED

- Under the Human Rights Act 1998, the UKSC has the power to decide whether an action by a public body or particular law is in breach of the ECHR.

- If it finds such a breach, it then issues a 'declaration of incompatibility'. This effectively requires the action to be reversed, as the government institution or public body concerned is breaking its own rules by not following the principles set out in the ECHR.
- Although it is obliged to respect the precedents of the ECtHR, on rare occasions the UKSC has effectively sent cases back to Strasbourg for reconsideration, e.g. the **Horncastle case** in 2009.
- The Horncastle case influenced the ECtHR when it came to hear a similar case 2 years later. Therefore, the UKSC is both influenced by and influences the ECtHR.
- Separate to the ECHR, the UKSC must also take EU law into consideration when hearing cases that concern European treaties to which the UK is signed up. It can also refer cases to the European Court of Justice in Luxembourg for a final verdict.
- Brexit will impact only on the UKSC and EU law, *not* the UKSC and the ECHR.

> **Horncastle case** This case concerned the use of statements from witnesses not present in court and therefore unable to be cross-examined. Long accepted in British courts, the ECtHR ruled that a person convicted by such hearsay evidence had been denied access to a fair trial. The UKSC in effect disagreed.

Appointment procedure

REVISED

- Designed to be non-political, independent and based on merit alone.
- Vacancies are filled by a special selection commission.
- The selection commission is made up of the president and deputy president of the court, and a member each from the Judicial Appointments Commission, the Judicial Appointments Board for Scotland and the Northern Ireland Judicial Appointments Commission. This reflects the fact that the court oversees the courts in all parts of the UK.
- The commission consults with certain senior judges (who do not wish to be appointed themselves) before putting forward a name selected on merit alone.
- The lord chancellor can accept or reject the nomination. They cannot put forward their own candidate.

Key cases

REVISED

Table 4.3 outlines some key cases that have been heard by the UKSC.

Table 4.3 A selection of key cases heard by the UKSC

Case	Key features	Outcome and significance
Al Rawi and others (Respondents) v *The Security Service and others* (Appellants) [2011]	<ul><li>In certain terrorist trials, were the UK security services allowed to give evidence in secret?</li><li>Should protecting national security trump the long-held British legal principle of open justice?</li><li>A case concerning both human rights (to a fair trial) and the extent of government powers to alter normal judicial procedures.</li></ul>	<ul><li>A defeat for the UK government.</li><li>The court believed that even in such serious cases, each side must hear and see all the evidence and arguments put before the judge by the other side.</li><li>A victory for supporters of open and transparent justice.</li></ul>
Trump International Golf Club Limited and another (Appellants) v *Scottish Ministers* (Respondents) [2015]	<ul><li>Had the Scottish government exceeded its powers in allowing a wind farm to be built near a new golf club owned by one of Donald Trump's businesses?</li><li>An *ultra vires* case.</li></ul>	<ul><li>The court found in favour of the Scottish government.</li><li>The Scottish government had not exceeded its powers.</li></ul>

Case	Key features	Outcome and significance
R (on the application of Shindler and another) (Appellants) v *Chancellor of the Duchy of Lancaster and another* (Respondents) [2016]	● Should UK citizens who had lived abroad for over 15 years be allowed to vote in the EU (Brexit) referendum? ● A case about human rights in the area of politics and elections, and the right to vote.	● The ruling confirmed the decision that UK voting regulations did not unlawfully interfere with the right of freedom of movement within the EU. ● A ruling that went in favour of the government.
R (on the application of Miller and Dos Santos) (Respondents) v *Secretary of State for Exiting the European Union* (Appellant) [2017] The **Article 50** 'Brexit' Appeal	● Must the government get parliamentary approval to invoke Article 50 to leave the EU following the EU referendum? ● Must the devolved assemblies be consulted about Article 50? ● A case about important constitutional matters.	● Parliament must be allowed a vote on Article 50. ● Devolved assemblies need not be consulted on Article 50. ● The case reinforced the principle of parliamentary sovereignty and the supremacy of Westminster over devolved assemblies in such matters. ● In part a victory and in part a defeat for the government. ● Not a pro-Remain decision by the court, rather about interpreting the British constitution.
Great Ormond Street Hospital v *Yates and Gard* [2017] The Charlie Gard case	● Were the parents of a seriously ill baby (Charlie Gard) allowed to take him abroad for medical treatment? ● The removal was opposed by both Great Ormond Street Hospital and Charlie's independent guardian on the legal grounds it was not in his best interests. ● A case involving medical ethics to some extent, but actually more about the legality of the procedures followed.	● The court found against Charlie's parents who were not allowed to take him to the USA. ● He died shortly afterwards when his life support was removed. ● The case reaffirmed the principle that parents do not have the ultimate say on their child's care. ● Although involving a matter of life and death, the case was not about morality or ethics but interpretation of the law and legal procedures.
Commissioner of Police of the Metropolis (Appellant) v *DSD and another* (Respondents) [2018] The John Worboys ('black cab rapist') case	● Two victims of the serial rapist John Worboys successfully won a case against the Metropolitan Police for not taking their allegations seriously enough at the time. ● They won substantial compensation. ● A human rights case.	● The UKSC decided that the victims' human rights had been breached. ● If a police force conducts an investigation into a major crime which fails in a sufficiently serious way, it could be liable to a human rights action brought by the victim.

Revision activity

Create a diagram that shows the respective powers of the UKSC, the ECtHR and the European Court of Justice and where they overlap and where they are separate.

Article 50 The process by which a member state can leave the European Union.

Now test yourself

TESTED

5 Are UKSC judges appointed in the same way as other judges?
6 Explain the difference between EU law and the ECHR.
7 Where is the ECtHR located?
8 Must the British government accept all the decisions of the ECtHR?
9 What is the link between the UKSC and EU law/the ECHR?
10 On the whole, does the UKSC tend to support or oppose the UK government in its judgements?

Answers on p. 110

Impact on government, legislature and the making of policy

REVISED

The UKSC acts as a significant check and balance on government and parliament in regard to both legislation and executive actions.

Under the Human Rights Act 1998, all government bills must include a statement saying that, in the minister's view, the bill is either compatible with human rights or that it is incompatible but that the government nevertheless wishes to proceed with the bill. The UKSC may, of course, disagree in a subsequent court case that the bill was compatible. This makes governments more careful and cautious when drawing up bills.

On rare occasions, the UK government can choose to ignore the rulings of the ECtHR. In 2005, the court ruled that a blanket ban on denying all prisoners the vote was incompatible with the ECHR, but parliament did not subsequently change the law.

Sometimes, the court comes close to overturning key aspects of government policy. For example, in 2015 the UKSC only narrowly (by a 3 to 2 margin) upheld the controversial cap on the total amount of benefits an out-of-work family can receive, including housing benefit and benefits for children, to £500 per week. Opponents claimed it breached aspects of both the ECHR and the UN Convention on the Rights of a Child. Had the opponents won, it would have created a major headache for the government and seriously threatened the principles of both parliamentary sovereignty and democratic accountability.

One of the US Founding Fathers, Alexander Hamilton, wrote that the judiciary would always be the least dangerous branch of government, controlling 'neither the sword nor the purse', but may be increasingly influential. This seems to be true of the UKSC as it becomes increasingly prominent in policy making and implementation.

> **Exam tip**
>
> Make sure you learn a small number of key cases where the UKSC has made important decisions. Ensure you know what category each falls under (e.g. human rights, the power of government etc.). Use the internet and media to keep examples up to date.

Summary

You should now have an understanding of:
- the meaning of the following key terms: judicial independence, judicial impartiality/neutrality, the separation of powers, *ultra vires* and judicial review
- how judges, including those of the UK Supreme Court, are appointed, and issues concerning the composition of the judiciary
- how the UK Supreme Court impacts on both government and parliament

Exam practice

AS

1 Explain the importance of a judicial review. [6]
2 'The British judiciary has become increasingly influential in recent years.' Analyse and evaluate this statement. [25]

A-level

3 Explain and analyse three key aspects of the UK judiciary. [9]
4 'The UKSC has become increasingly prominent and powerful in the political life of the nation.' Analyse and evaluate this statement. [25]

Answers and quick quiz 4 online

ONLINE

5 Devolution

Key points

- Since 1999, the way the UK is run has been transformed by devolution.
- Devolution is the delegation of power from the UK Parliament in Westminster to assemblies in Cardiff (Wales) and Belfast (Northern Ireland) and the Scottish Parliament in Edinburgh.
- The Westminster Parliament is technically still able to pass laws for any part of the UK, but in practice only deals with devolved matters with the agreement of the devolved governments.

> **Typical mistake**
>
> Devolution is not the same as federalism, where power is permanently transferred to regional assemblies or states, as in the USA. In theory, Westminster could take back the powers of the devolved assemblies.

Devolved bodies in the UK

Roles, powers and responsibilities of devolved bodies

The extent of these powers varies somewhat from region to region, as shown in Table 5.1.

Table 5.1 Current UK devolved bodies and their powers

Devolved body	Location	Number of members	Voting system	Key powers (selected examples)	Examples of areas where it lacks powers	Leader of the government (mid-2018)
Scottish Parliament	Edinburgh	128	Additional Member System (AMS)	Agriculture Environment Income tax Education Health Transport Justice, policing and courts	Foreign policy Brexit negotiations Defence and national security Trade and industry	Nicola Sturgeon (SNP)
National Assembly for Wales	Cardiff	60	AMS	Agriculture Environment Education Health Transport Fire and rescue services	Foreign policy Brexit negotiations Defence and national security	Carwyn Jones (Labour)

→

Devolved body	Location	Number of members	Voting system	Key powers (selected examples)	Examples of areas where it lacks powers	Leader of the government (mid-2018)
Northern Ireland Assembly*	Belfast (Stormont)	90	Single Transferable Vote (STV)	Agriculture Environment Education Health Transport Enterprise, trade and investment	Income tax Foreign policy Brexit negotiations Defence and national security	Currently vacant due to suspension of the Assembly since early 2017

* As part of the Good Friday Agreement, uniquely in Ulster executive power must be shared between the two largest parties, i.e. a unionist and a nationalist party. This is to avoid power being held solely by the majority community. The clause is designed to avoid sectarian discrimination and ensure power is shared between the two communities.

Key dates

REVISED

1997 Tony Blair's Labour government holds referendums in Scotland and Wales over devolution. Both vote in favour, albeit by a very small margin in Wales.

1998 The Good Friday Agreement leads to a ceasefire and an end to **the Troubles** in Northern Ireland, paving the way for a Northern Ireland Assembly.

1999 Devolved assemblies are set up in Wales and Scotland.

2011 A referendum in Wales supports the transfer of greater powers by a large margin (63% to 37%).

2012 The Scotland Act devolves some tax-raising powers (e.g. income tax) to the Scottish Parliament and allows it to borrow up to £2 billion a year.

2014 Scotland rejects full independence in a referendum (55% to 45%). The Wales Act grants more powers to the Welsh government including **stamp duty**, business rates and landfill tax.

2016 The Scotland Act devolves further powers including control over road signs and onshore oil extraction, and to change its electoral system, with a two-thirds vote by the Scottish Parliament.

2017 The Northern Ireland Assembly is suspended due to a breakdown in relations between the two largest parties, the DUP (unionist) and Sinn Fein (nationalist).
The Wales Act gives further powers to Cardiff, largely similar to those granted to Scotland in 2016 but excluding the power to set income tax rates/bands.

> **The Troubles** The period from the late 1960s when much of Northern Ireland was affected by terrorism including bombings and assassinations carried out by terrorists from both communities who belonged to groups such as the Provisional IRA or the Ulster Defence Association (UDA).
>
> **Stamp duty** A tax payable when buying property.

> **Exam tip**
>
> Given the extent of powers now in the hands of the devolved assemblies, the UK system of government can be referred to as quasi-federal rather than unitary.

Devolution in England

England is the only region of the UK not to have devolved assemblies. Instead, it has various tiers of local government with different degrees of power and responsibility.

Local government

- Single-tier **unitary authorities** carry out all functions of local government. These are mostly in large cities and urban areas such as Birmingham and Portsmouth.
- Two-tier local councils comprise county councils and district councils. Here, functions are split between the two types of local authority. They are found mainly in more rural and less densely populated areas.
- Among the key functions of English local government are education, providing social care, waste collection and the provision of social housing.
- Some large cities or regions (Greater Manchester, Liverpool City Region, West Midlands, West of England, Tees Valley, Sheffield City Region and Cambridgeshire and Peterborough) now have directly elected 'metro mayors' who serve several combined local authorities. The government's Devolution Deals allow combined authorities to take on additional responsibilities, but require a metro mayor to be elected for that area.

> **Unitary authorities** Where a single council carries out all the functions of local authorities, including major ones such as education and social care undertaken elsewhere by county councils.

> **Typical mistake**
>
> Don't confuse the seven metro mayors and the traditional mayors councils have already. Metro mayors are combined authority mayors who are voted for by the electorate in the area. Traditional mayors hold office only for one year and the post is ceremonial with no decision-making powers.

Limits on local government

Unlike the devolved assemblies, local councils are severely limited in what they can do on their own initiative:

- They have very limited legislative powers, although they can, in some circumstances, introduce certain measures such as congestion charges in London.
- Most functions that involve carrying out responsibilities and roles are decided by central government.
- Most revenue raising is tightly controlled by central government. For example, council tax cannot be raised beyond a limit set by Westminster (5% in 2018).

Debate around devolution for England

With the rise of devolved assemblies elsewhere in the UK, there has been some discussion around whether there should be an English Parliament or regional assemblies, as shown in Table 5.2.

Table 5.2 Arguments for and against an English Parliament or regional assemblies

Arguments for	Arguments against
<ul><li>It would be a logical extension of the creation of devolved assemblies, which on the whole have worked well and proved popular.</li><li>It would bring parity across the UK regarding devolution.</li></ul>	<ul><li>England lacks the national identity of Scotland, Wales or Northern Ireland.</li><li>There is no widespread support for such a measure. A referendum in 2004 to set up an elected assembly for the northeast was decisively rejected 78% to 22%.</li></ul>

→

Arguments for	Arguments against
• Regional assemblies would enable decision making to be brought closer to voters and reduce the dominance of London. • An English Parliament would resolve the West Lothian question whereby Scottish, Welsh and Northern Ireland MPs currently have a vote on matters that affect only England, whereas MPs from England are unable to vote on matters that have been devolved. • An English Parliament could be located away from the capital (Birmingham?) and thus reduce London's current dominance of politics and the media. • It would allow an alternative electoral system to be used, as is the case elsewhere in the UK, and therefore resolve the issue of electoral reform.	• England is much larger in terms of population than any of the other regions. No other country with a federal or semi-federal system has one region that is so dominant within the whole nation. • Regional assemblies would add extra cost and bureaucracy to the UK political system. • There are other ways of resolving the West Lothian question such as English votes for English laws (EVEL). Here, an extra stage is introduced in the middle of the law-making process, allowing English MPs to block anything they don't like in bills deemed to be 'England only'. • An English Parliament would raise the issue of what is the role and purpose of the Westminster Parliament, which could lead to more conflict between the UK and English prime ministers. • Electoral reform is a separate issue and English devolution should not be created just to achieve it.

Now test yourself

TESTED ☐

1 Look at the following statements about devolution in the UK and decide whether they are true or false.
   (a) The devolved assemblies all have equal powers.
   (b) Devolution in Northern Ireland is slightly different to that in Scotland and Wales.
   (c) Devolution has seen more powers transferred away from Westminster over the last 20 or so years.
   (d) English local government represents a form of devolution.
   (e) Devolved assemblies use different electoral systems to those used for UK general elections.
2 What is the West Lothian question?
3 Which sort of places are likely to have unitary authorities?
4 What does EVEL stand for?
5 Name a region that has a directly elected metro mayor.
6 What were held before devolution was introduced?

Answers on p. 110

Revision activity

Using the arguments for and against further devolution for England, together with any other relevant points from your own notes, create two word maps that show the relative importance of points on each side of the argument.

Exam tip

Ensure you distinguish between proposals for a single English Parliament and for a number of English regional assemblies. Both come under the heading of English devolution, but they are different approaches.

The impact of devolution on the UK government

Key points

REVISED ☐

• Devolution has reduced the power of Westminster, as many areas of government are now the responsibility of devolved assemblies.
• It raises the issue of English devolution and the West Lothian question.
• It has led the government to transfer more powers to some English local authorities via combined authorities and metro mayors.
• It has not weakened (in theory at least) the concept of Westminster sovereignty. Devolved assemblies have their powers delegated not inalienably transferred. In reality, however, it is highly unlikely that devolution would ever be reversed.

- It has created more variation across the UK. For example, prescriptions are free in Wales and Scotland and those earning over £150,000 pay 1% more income tax in Scotland.

Summary

You should now have an understanding of:

- the current structure and powers of local government/devolution in England
- how devolution has developed and expanded since 1997
- the main powers of the devolved assemblies

in Scotland, Wales and Northern Ireland
- the arguments for and against further devolution in England and setting up an English Parliament
- how the devolved assemblies have affected the Westminster Parliament

Exam practice

AS

1 Explain the importance of any one devolved assembly in the UK. [6]
2 'The case for an English Parliament is overwhelming.' Analyse and evaluate this statement. [25]

A-level

3 'Devolution in the UK has been a resounding success.' Analyse and evaluate this statement. [25]

Read the following extract.

Although introduced with high hopes of stemming a growing tide of support for independence in the regions, devolution has since its introduction led to unforeseen problems. Arguably, it has had the opposite effect and actually stimulated demands for separation; the Scottish independence referendum is a case in point. Scotland only voted to stay within the UK by a narrow margin and subsequent reforms have offered Scotland even more powers, which will surely push it closer to outright independence. Fiscal powers have also been unwisely used to create a different tax regime to that in the rest of the UK. This has led to inequality and divergence within the UK. It could be argued, though, that this simply reflects the different political traditions and views across the different parts of the UK.

In Northern Ireland the outcomes have also been less positive. Although the 'peace dividend' has been an undoubted asset, by 2018 the Northern Ireland Assembly appeared stubbornly stuck in a standoff between the two communities. For many, direct rule from Westminster looks like the only alternative in the medium term. In addition, the Stormont government enjoys fewer powers than its counterparts in Edinburgh and Cardiff.

The real pitfall, however, is the lack of serious consideration of devolution for England itself. If devolution were ever to have worked fairly and effectively from the start, an English Parliament should have been introduced as part of a full not partial package in creating a quasi-federal state.

Source: Original material, 2018

4 Analyse, evaluate and compare the arguments in the above extract for and against the view that devolution has worked poorly in the UK. [25]

Answers and quick quiz 5 online

ONLINE

6 Democracy and participation

Key points

- The UK is a representative democracy.
- Before 1918, all women and many men could not vote. Groups such as the Chartists, the Suffragists and the Suffragettes campaigned for change. Today, there are demands for voting rights for prisoners and 16- and 17-year-olds.
- In a healthy democracy, people vote in elections, join political parties and engage politically with important issues. Some fear that modern Britain is experiencing a participation crisis (Table 6.5) as fewer people are getting involved in politics.

> **Democracy** A system of government in which the people have ultimate power. The term 'democracy' means 'rule by the people'.
>
> **Direct democracy** A system of democracy in which the people make decisions, not the government. Votes take place on specific questions.

Democracy

Nature of democracy

The word **democracy** comes from the Greek words *demos* ('the people') and *kratia* ('rule by'). The concept of 'rule by the people' originated in Greece around the fifth century BC. Athenians used **direct democracy** but modern Western democracies use **representative democracy**.

Table 6.1 outlines the features of democracy.

> **Representative democracy** A system of democracy in which people vote for elected representatives. Elected representatives make decisions on the people's behalf.

Table 6.1 The features of democracy

Feature	Description
Representation	People's opinions are represented to the government.
Participation	People participate in politics. This can be through voting, joining political parties or pressure groups, or lobbying their elected representatives or the government.
Accountability	The government is accountable to the people. If the electorate think the government has done a bad job, it can vote in a different government.
Legitimacy	The government has legitimacy (legal authority) because it has been chosen by the people.
Rule of law	The country's laws apply equally to everyone and anyone who breaks the law is punished.
Elections	People vote regularly in elections. These may be to elect representatives (representative democracy) or to directly decide on specific issues (direct democracy).
Smooth transition of power	There is a formal process for handing power from one government to the next and this takes place peacefully.
Civil rights	People have their rights protected by law.
Education and information	The public are politically educated and have access to accurate information from trustworthy sources.

Different types of democracy

Direct democracy

- Direct democracy means that people vote 'yes' or 'no' on specific questions.
- This is different from representative democracy, in which people vote for representatives to make decisions on their behalf.
- No modern country makes every decision using direct democracy. This would be too difficult with big populations.
- Switzerland has the most directly democratic system. Its citizens vote frequently on a wide range of questions and they can propose initiatives to change the law. The USA also uses initiatives.
- Elements of direct democracy are used increasingly in the UK, including referendums and petitions.

Table 6.2 compares the advantages and disadvantages of direct democracy.

> **Revision activity**
>
> Using the information given in Table 7.9 (pp. 70–71), on the 2016 EU referendum, add examples for each of the advantages and disadvantages listed in Table 6.2.

Table 6.2 **Advantages and disadvantages of direct democracy**

Advantages	Disadvantages
• People can participate directly in the decision-making process. • The wishes of the people cannot be ignored by their elected representatives or the government. • People can be motivated to become well-informed about political issues. • Decisions have the direct authority of the people. This gives them greater legitimacy.	• The public may not fully understand the question they are voting on. Elected representatives might be better placed to analyse and evaluate the issue. • The majority of people may vote for something that undermines the rights of a minority group. This is known as the tyranny of the majority. • People may vote for emotional or populist short-term reasons, rather than taking a more considered view. • Holding so many votes is slow and expensive, particularly in countries with large populations.

Representative government

- Almost all modern Western democracies use representative government.
- Regular elections are held so that people can elect representatives.
- In the UK there are separate national and local elections.
- These elected representatives become part of a legislative assembly.
- A government is also elected, either directly (as in a **presidential democracy** like the USA) or indirectly (as in a **parliamentary democracy** like the UK).
- Some elected representatives follow the delegate model (see p. 21) in which they vote according to how they think their constituents would wish them to.
- Others follow the trustee model (see p. 21) developed by Edmund Burke (1729–97), who argued that MPs should vote according to their best judgement, as they have a better understanding of the issues than their constituents.
- Most Western representative democracies are **liberal democracies**.

> **Presidential democracy**
> A democracy in which the executive (government) is directly elected by the people.
>
> **Parliamentary democracy**
> A democracy in which the executive is not directly elected by the people. Instead, the executive is formed by whichever party has the greatest support in the legislature (parliament).
>
> **Liberal democracies** Types of representative democracy in which the rule of law is followed, the freedom of citizens is protected by the government and many different political parties compete freely to win power.

> **Typical mistake**
>
> Don't assume that the UK's use of referendums makes it a direct democracy, rather than a representative democracy. It remains a representative democracy in which MPs are elected to make decisions on the people's behalf. The increasing use of referendums since 1997 (see Table 7.9) means that the UK has become a more participatory democracy (one in which the public participate actively in decision making).

1 What does 'democracy' mean?
2 Name as many features of democracy as you can.
3 What is the difference between direct democracy and representative democracy?
4 Give two examples of modern Western democracies that use elements of direct democracy.
5 What are the advantages and disadvantages of representative democracy?

Answers on p. 110

Exam tip

Make sure you fully understand the different types of democracy and how they apply to the UK. You can make synoptic links from all the other topics on the specification to democracy (e.g. pressure groups and pluralism, parliament and representative democracy, the EU and direct democracy), so be prepared to use democracy as a synoptic link in other questions on the UK exam paper.

How suffrage has changed since the Great Reform Act 1832

REVISED

Suffrage is the right to vote, also referred to as the franchise. Table 6.3 summarises how suffrage has changed in the UK.

Table 6.3 **How has suffrage changed in the UK?**

Key date and Act	Significance
Before 1832	Only rich male landowners could vote
	Fewer than 4% of the population
Great Reform Act 1832	One in five male adults could vote
	5.6% of the total population
Second Reform Act 1867	Much bigger in scope than the Great Reform Act
	Allowed working-class men in cities to vote if they met a property qualification
	Doubled the size of the electorate
Third Reform Act 1887	All working men who met a property qualification could vote
	40% of adult men still excluded
Representation of the People Act 1918	A product of the social and political changes caused by the First World War
	All men over the age of 21 (or 19 for veterans) could vote
	Women over 30 who met the property qualification could vote
Representation of the People Act 1928	Women finally received the vote on equal terms to men
	All men and women over 21 could vote
	Property qualifications removed
Representation of the People Act 1969	Voting age lowered to 18

Typical mistake

Don't claim that women won the vote in 1918; the reality was rather more complicated. *Some* women (those over 30 who met the property qualification) won the vote in 1918, but the rest had to wait until 1928 to receive the franchise on the same terms as men.

Debates regarding universal suffrage

Gender

- Women were traditionally seen as 'the weaker sex', both physically and mentally.
- They were not considered to have sufficient education or intelligence to be trusted with the vote.
- Opponents of women's suffrage in the nineteenth and early twentieth centuries argued that women were too emotional to vote rationally.
- Traditionalists felt that a woman's place was in the home, tending to her family. Politics would distract her.

Class

- The wealthy elite who held the franchise before 1832 worried that their power would be reduced if people from other classes had the vote.
- There were fears that working-class men were too poorly educated to understand political issues.
- Some feared the working class would support socialism, threatening the economic welfare of other classes.
- The contribution and sacrifice of working-class men during the First World War meant that denying them the vote could no longer be justified.

Ethnicity

- There were (and are) no ethnic qualifications for voting in the UK.

Age

- Younger people were not seen as having sufficient political education, independence or maturity. People aged 18 to 20 years old only received the vote in 1969.
- Young women aged 21 to 29 were denied the vote in 1918, despite their contribution to the war effort. They were considered more emotional and unstable than older women.
- Today, there is a campaign to give 16- and 17-year-olds the vote.
- 16- and 17-year-olds were allowed to vote in the 2014 Scottish independence referendum, as it was recognised that the referendum result would affect the rest of their lives. They had a higher turnout than 18- to 24-year-olds.
- 16- and 17-year-olds can vote in elections for the Scottish Parliament and councils. They will soon be able to vote in Welsh local elections.
- The Labour Party, the Scottish National Party (SNP), the Liberal Democrats, Plaid Cymru and the Green Party all support the Votes at 16 campaign, as does the Electoral Reform Society.

Revision activities

1 Make two lists: one giving arguments in favour of 16- and 17-year-olds having the vote, and one giving arguments against.
2 Should 16- and 17-year-olds be given the vote? Write a paragraph to summarise your opinion.

Exam tip

In a question on the development of suffrage, make sure you emphasise the importance of class as well as gender. Many working-class men were excluded from the franchise until 1918, just as women were.

Significance of Chartists, Suffragists and Suffragettes

Table 6.4 outlines the significance of three groups: Chartists, Suffragists and Suffragettes.

Table 6.4 Chartists, Suffragists and Suffragettes

Group	Methods	Significance
Chartists (1838–48)	• The Chartist movement was set up after the Great Reform Act 1832. • They campaigned for votes for all men over 21, secret ballots, no property qualifications for MPs, pay for MPs, equal size constituencies and yearly elections to parliament. • The movement presented three petitions signed by millions to parliament.	• All three petitions were rejected by parliament. • Authorities dealt harshly with unrest provoked by the rejection of petitions. • The movement lacked a single leader and struggled to coordinate different groups across the nation. • Some Chartists called for violence, which caused many middle-class supporters to leave the movement, resulting in less money for campaigning. • The movement died out but the Second and Third Reform Acts were passed in 1867 and 1887. • Today, all the Chartists' aims have been met apart from yearly elections.
Suffragists (1860s–1918)	• Suffragists had been campaigning for the vote since the 1860s. • In 1897 they formed the National Union of Women's Suffrage Societies (NUWSS). • Suffragists campaigned for the vote using peaceful constitutional methods (e.g. petitions, speeches, marches and letter-writing).	• Despite decades of campaigning, women were no closer to getting the vote by 1903, which resulted in the formation of the Suffragettes. • The NUWSS had more than 100,000 members by 1914. • Leader Millicent Fawcett said their movement was 'like a glacier, slow-moving but unstoppable'.
Suffragettes (1903–14)	• Frustrated with the Suffragists' lack of progress, Emmeline Pankhurst formed a rival organisation, the Women's Social and Political Union (WSPU), in 1903. • Suffragettes used militant methods including window breaking, chaining themselves to railings and arson. • Suffragettes received harsh prison sentences, which they attempted to reduce by hunger striking. • Emily Davison was killed in 1913 when she intercepted the king's horse at the Derby. • Leader Christabel Pankhurst went into hiding in France to avoid arrest. • The movement called off their campaign when war broke out in 1914.	• Suffragettes were dealt with harshly by the police and the government, including being force-fed in prison. • They attracted national attention and coverage in newspapers. • They were criticised by the Suffragists for using increasingly extreme methods. • The government refused to 'give in' to violence. • Many key supporters left the movement in protest over the arson campaign; membership numbers and funding fell. • Some argue that women won the vote in 1918 through their war service, not because of the Suffragettes. • It is likely that the government was eager to avoid a return to violence when they enfranchised women in 1918.

Typical mistake

Don't confuse the Chartists with Suffragists or Suffragettes. The Chartists were a mid-nineteenth century group that campaigned for male suffrage, whereas both the Suffragists and Suffragettes campaigned for female suffrage. The Suffragists date from the 1860s, whereas the Suffragettes, who were prepared to use much more militant methods, date from 1903.

Suffrage as a human right

- In 2005 the European Court of Human Rights ruled that denying all prisoners the right to vote violated their human rights.
- The case in question, *Hirst* v *UK* [2005], involved a prisoner, John Hirst, who was serving a sentence for manslaughter. He argued that the UK government was in breach of the Human Rights Act 1998, which incorporated the European Convention on Human Rights into UK law. The case was initially dismissed by the UK High Court, but Hirst appealed to the European Court of Human Rights where he was successful. The UK government did not comply with the ruling.
- Pressure groups such as the Howard League for Penal Reform have campaigned for the government to obey the court's ruling.
- Legally, the court has made it clear that voting is a human right.
- However, many people believe that voting is a privilege that should be removed if someone commits a crime.
- In 2017 the Conservative government announced plans to allow a small number of prisoners to vote (around 100) in order to compromise with the European Court of Human Rights.

Now test yourself

TESTED

6 In which year did Britain first have universal suffrage?
7 Name the Chartists' six demands.
8 What was the main difference between the Suffragists and the Suffragettes?
9 Which political parties support the Votes at 16 campaign?

Answers on pp. 110–111

Participation

Is there a participation crisis?

REVISED

Participation is crucial to any democracy, but the UK may be experiencing a participation crisis (Table 6.5).

Table 6.5 Arguments for and against a participation crisis

Arguments for	Arguments against
• Turnout in general elections has fallen in recent decades. In 1950 more than 80% of the electorate voted. In 2001 just 59% did, a record low. • Some elections had even worse turnout — in the 2012 Police and Crime Commissioner (PCC) elections, just 15% of the electorate voted. • Party membership has fallen since the 1950s, when the Conservatives had more than 2.5 million members and the Labour Party more than 1 million. In 2018 the Conservatives had just 124,000 members.	• Turnout in general elections has been rising since 2001, reaching 69% in the 2017 general election. • Turnout in recent referendums has also been high. Some 85% voted in the 2014 Scottish independence referendum and 72% in the 2016 EU referendum. • The contrast between the PCC elections and the EU and Scottish referendums shows that the electorate is selective: if people care about an issue, they will participate.

Participation People's involvement in political activity. It includes voting, writing to an MP, joining a political party or pressure group, standing for office, protesting and signing a petition.

→

Arguments for	Arguments against	Typical mistake
● **Partisan dealignment** means that people increasingly feel no affiliation to any political party. ● **Trade unions** have fewer members and are less powerful than in the 1980s. ● Political apathy appears to be commonplace among young people. Turnout data for 18- to 24-year-olds show they are less politically engaged than any other age group. ● Disillusionment with politicians has increased since the 2009 expenses scandal. ● 'Slacktivism' describes the tendency for people to participate in a superficial way by 'liking' or sharing political content online.	● The membership of some parties is increasing: Labour has more than 500,000 members and the SNP membership more than quadrupled following the 2014 independence referendum, reaching a high of 125,000 in 2018. ● New parties has done very well in recent years: the SNP, UKIP and the Greens have all made electoral progress. ● Pressure group membership has increased. ● Social media and the internet have changed the nature of political participation. Pressure groups and political parties use social media to reach the public, coordinate their campaigns and raise money. ● Internet-based movements can be powerful: the #MeToo campaign against sexual harassment led to a public debate and the resignation of defence secretary Michael Fallon in 2017.	Don't confuse class dealignment and partisan dealignment. Class dealignment is a trend for voting to be less dependent on class. In the 1950s, middle-class voters tended to vote Conservative and working-class voters Labour, but they are now less closely aligned. Partisan dealignment is the process by which individuals are less likely to support a political party at all.

Exam tip

Examiners are looking for detailed examples, so be sure to learn the most recent turnout and membership figures. Your analysis will be much stronger if you support it with evidence.

Partisan dealignment The process by which the electorate have become less strongly affiliated to political parties. It is reflected by falling party membership numbers.

Trade unions Organisations made up of workers, which campaign for better working conditions.

Increasing participation

REVISED

Suggested methods for increasing participation include:
● votes at 16
● online voting
● compulsory voting
● changing the electoral system so that everyone's vote counts equally
● adopting a proportional electoral system, which would benefit minor parties and give voters more choice
● increasing political education in schools
● reducing the membership fees of political parties
● more direct democracy

Revision activity

Read the suggestions for increasing political participation. Make a note of the advantages and disadvantages for each. Rank the suggestions in order of effectiveness (start with the one you think would be the most effective).

Now test yourself

10 How have methods of participation changed in recent years?
11 What is meant by partisan dealignment?
12 What is meant by 'slacktivism'?
13 Which two political parties have seen significant membership growth in recent years?
14 What was the turnout for the 2012 PCC elections?

Answers on p. 111

Summary

You should now have an understanding of:
- the nature of democracy, including its key features
- the difference between direct and representative democracy
- how the franchise has been extended from 1832 to the present
- historical debates regarding who should have the vote and the modern debate over Votes at 16
- the significance of the Chartists, Suffragists and Suffragettes in campaigning for increased suffrage
- the controversy over whether voting is a human right
- how to justify whether you think prisoners should be allowed to vote
- the extent to which the UK has a participation crisis
- suggestions as to how participation levels could be increased

Exam practice

AS

Read the following extracts.

Extract 1

Internet-based campaigning has led to the rise of 'slacktivists', online activists who 'like', 'tweet' and 'share' from the comfort of their sofas but take no real action for the causes that they claim to support. Political party membership has become the preserve of an increasingly eccentric few. Most young people who claim to be politically engaged are merely spectators and commentators. Few bother to attend protests or marches. Many do not even bother to vote.

Source: Original material, 2018

Extract 2

Politics has been transformed by social media and the internet. It has never been so easy for the public to contact MPs, simply by emailing or even tweeting them. Campaigns can grow quickly using e-petitions and indeed parliament has recognised this by agreeing to debate any petition on its website that reaches 100,000 signatures. Political videos can go viral and so can movements, as the success of #MeToo proved in 2017. Political parties use the internet to contact their supporters cheaply and efficiently, and sites like Facebook to recruit new members. Some have done this more effectively than others. In 2017 the size of Jeremy Corbyn's Twitter following far exceeded those of the other leaders of UK parties and Labour had over half a million members at a time when the Conservative Party would not even agree to release its membership figures. Most encouraging of all is the fact that online campaigning offers parties and campaigns the chance to engage young voters who have traditionally been more difficult to mobilise than other age groups.

Source: Original material, 2018

1 Analyse, evaluate and compare the arguments presented in both of the above extracts concerning participation. [12]
2 'The UK already has universal suffrage: no further extension of the franchise is required.' Analyse and evaluate this statement. [25]

A-level

3 Explain and analyse three ways in which the Suffragettes were significant in the campaign to extend the franchise. [9]

Read the following extract.

In recent years, there has been much discussion of the phenomenon of partisan dealignment. It was argued that the falling membership figures of the main political parties were evidence of a long-term trend of political disengagement by the electorate. There is some truth to this: the membership figures of the Conservatives, for example, stood at 124,000 in 2018, a far cry from their 2.5 million members in the 1950s.

However, this analysis is over-simplistic. Firstly, it ignores the evidence that some smaller parties have seen significant increases in membership. UKIP had fewer than 15,000 members in 2008, and had more than doubled to 34,000 in 2017. From 2014 to 2016 the membership of the Scottish National Party (SNP) more than quadrupled. Furthermore, Labour has attracted more new members than any other party, its membership soaring from fewer than 190,000 in 2013 to more than 500,000 in 2017. It is clearly

possible, then, for a major party to attract large numbers of members, which contradicts the notion that the electorate are 'dealigning'.

It would be more logical to describe a state of 'partisan realignment', against a backdrop of class dealignment. Age, rather than class, has become the dominant factor that predicts how people will vote. This was the case in the 2014 Scottish independence referendum, the 2016 European Union referendum and the 2017 general election. It is notable that the parties that have seen significant membership gains have tended to attract support from a specific age-group (young people for Labour and the SNP, older people for UKIP). 1.7% of the electorate were members of a political party in 2017, compared to just 0.8% in 2013. While these figures have yet to return to the heights of 1983 (3.8%), the direction of travel is clear.

Source: Original material, 2018

4 Analyse, evaluate and compare the arguments in the above extract about partisan dealignment. [25]
5 'The UK is a thriving representative democracy.' Analyse and evaluate this statement. [25]

Answers and quick quiz 6 online

ONLINE

7 Elections and referendums

Key points

- Britain uses the first-past-the-post (FPTP) electoral system in general elections, but it has significant weaknesses.
- Alternative voting systems are used in other elections across the UK, with mixed results.
- Voting behaviour in general elections is influenced by a wide range of different factors, as revealed by three election case studies.
- Referendums have been used more frequently since 1998, though debates continue as to their impact on democracy.

Electoral systems

First-past-the-post

- A plurality system in which the electorate votes for one candidate in their constituency.
- Whichever candidate gets the most votes wins.
- Candidates do not need to win a majority of votes cast.
- Used in general elections in the UK to elect representatives (MPs) to the House of Commons.

Table 7.1 outlines the advantages and disadvantages of the FPTP system.

Table 7.1 **The advantages and disadvantages of FPTP**

	Advantages	Disadvantages
Voting	<ul><li>Simple: voters put an X next to their preferred candidate.</li><li>Easy to understand: whoever gets the most votes wins the seat.</li></ul>	<ul><li>Millions of **wasted votes** nationally.</li><li>It encourages **tactical voting.**</li><li>The choice of candidate is made by the party, not the voter. If a voter wishes to vote Conservative, for example, they cannot choose between a selection of Conservative candidates.</li><li>Turnout tends to be lower in countries that use FPTP than in countries with proportional systems.</li></ul>
Constituencies	<ul><li>Each constituency is represented by one MP, so constituents know whom to contact.</li></ul>	<ul><li>A majority of voters in a constituency may have voted *against* their representative.</li><li>Voters in **safe seats** can feel that there is no point in voting if they do not support that party.</li><li>Election campaigns tend to ignore safe seats and focus instead on **marginal seats**.</li><li>In 2017 there were only 97 marginal seats (seats won by a margin of 5% or less of all votes), meaning that the vast majority of seats were uncompetitive.</li><li>Differing population sizes in constituencies mean that not all votes count equally: in 2017 the largest UK constituency was the Isle of Wight, with an electorate of 109,900; the smallest was Na h-Eileanan an Iar in Scotland, with an electorate of 21,200.</li></ul>

→

	Advantages	Disadvantages
Parties	<ul><li>FPTP tends to produce a two-party system, giving voters a clear choice between two broad parties, each of which has a realistic chance of forming a government.</li><li>Extremist parties find it difficult to win seats.</li></ul>	<ul><li>It favours parties with concentrated geographical support.</li><li>Minor parties win far fewer seats in the House of Commons than they would if seats were allocated proportionally to votes. In 2015 UKIP won just one seat for 3.9 million votes.</li><li>Minor parties struggle to convince supporters to vote for them, as their vote is likely to be wasted.</li><li>It is difficult for new parties to break into politics.</li></ul>
Governments	<ul><li>FPTP tends to result in majority single-party governments who find it easier to pass legislation.</li><li>Majority governments have a clear mandate for their manifestos.</li><li>Governments are easily held accountable by the electorate for implementing their manifestos.</li><li>Coalitions and minority governments are rare (seen as a good thing as they are traditionally weaker and less stable than majority governments).</li></ul>	<ul><li>FPTP exaggerates the mandate that governments actually have. In 1997 Labour won 2.5 times as many seats as the Conservatives, but only 1.4 times as many votes. This is known as a 'winner's bonus'.</li><li>Since 2010 the rise of minor and regional parties (particularly the Scottish National Party (SNP) since 2015) has made it difficult for either the Conservatives or Labour to win a large majority.</li><li>In effect, the UK now has a multi-party system but a voting system designed for two parties.</li><li>It does not guarantee strong majority governments. From 2010 to 2015, the UK had a coalition government, and a minority government from 2017.</li></ul>

Wasted votes Votes that do not contribute to the election of a political candidate. This includes votes for losing candidates and those for a winning candidate that are in excess of the threshold required for them to win the seat.

Tactical voting When a voter does not vote for their preferred party because they do not believe that party can win. Instead, they vote for another party that has a better chance of winning. This may be to stop a party they dislike from winning.

Safe seats Those in which one party has such a large majority that it is highly unlikely they could be won by another party.

Marginal seats Those in which the MPs' majority is small, meaning that they could easily be won by another party.

Typical mistake

Don't assume that the arguments against FPTP easily outweigh its benefits, as the reality is more complex. UK voters were offered the chance to change the voting system in the 2011 Alternative Vote referendum, but chose to keep FPTP. The main advantages of FPTP are its simplicity and the tendency to produce majority governments that the electorate can easily hold to account.

Now test yourself

TESTED ☐

1 What type of electoral system is FPTP?
2 What are wasted votes?
3 What is a winner's bonus?
4 What is a safe seat?

Answers on p. 111

Majoritarian and proportional electoral systems

Majoritarian systems are when a candidate needs to win 50% + 1 vote to win (an absolute majority). They are not proportional, so are likely to result in majority governments.

Proportional systems are when seats are allocated in proportion to the number of votes received by each party. They are likely to result in coalition governments.

Mixed systems involve two types of representatives, elected using different systems. Representatives of single-member constituencies are elected using a plurality or majoritarian system. Representatives of larger multi-member constituencies are elected using a proportional system.

These systems are explained in more detail in Table 7.2.

> **Regional list** A proportional system in which seats are allocated from votes using the d'Hondt formula. A closed list system is used: parties rank their candidates in the order that they will be elected and voters simply choose a party. Regional lists were used in UK elections to the European Parliament before the UK voted to leave the EU in the 2016 EU referendum.

Table 7.2 Alternatives to FPTP

	Majoritarian	Proportional	Mixed
Electoral system	Supplementary Vote (SV)	Single Transferable Vote (STV)	Additional Member System (AMS)
Where used	Elections for the mayor of London, directly elected metro mayors (see p. 47), police and crime commissioners	Northern Ireland elections	Elections to the Scottish Parliament, National Assembly for Wales, London Assembly
Features	<ul><li>A candidate needs to win 50% + 1 vote to win (an absolute majority).</li><li>Single-member constituencies.</li><li>Voters choose a first and second preference candidate.</li><li>If no candidate wins a majority from the first preferences, the second preferences of all but the top two candidates are counted.</li><li>The second preferences are added to the first preferences for the top two candidates to produce a winner.</li></ul>	<ul><li>Proportional representation (PR): seats are allocated in proportion to the number of votes received by each party.</li><li>Large multi-member constituencies.</li><li>Voters write numbers next to the candidates in order of their preference.</li><li>Candidates need a certain number of votes (the Droop quota) to win a seat.</li><li>Once a candidate meets the quota, their extra votes are reallocated to second preferences.</li><li>As candidates continue to meet the quota, remaining votes continue to be reallocated until all the seats are filled.</li></ul>	<ul><li>The greater proportion of seats in the legislature are elected using FPTP.</li><li>A smaller proportion of seats are allocated using proportional representation.</li><li>The FPTP seats represent single-member constituencies.</li><li>The **regional list** seats represent larger multi-member constituencies.</li></ul>

→

	Majoritarian	Proportional	Mixed
Advantages	• Increased legitimacy: representatives need to command broader support than under FPTP. • Choice: voters can vote for minor parties with their first preference and use their second preference for whichever front-runner they would most like to win.	• Proportional: voters can support minor parties knowing their vote will count. • Greatest choice: using STV, voters can choose both the party and the individual candidate.	• Choice: voters can confidently vote for minor parties with their regional list vote. • Split-ticket voting allows voters to choose one party for their constituency vote, and a different party for their list vote. • Constituency seats retain the relationship between the MP and the constituency.
Disadvantages	• Not proportional. • Very difficult for minor parties to win, although they may receive support at the first preference stage. • Votes for anyone other than the two main candidates are still wasted. • Despite being a majoritarian system, it is possible for the winner to be elected without a majority. • Can result in the election of the 'least worst' candidate rather than the best (the ultimate winner may not have won the first preference vote).	• Coalition governments are highly likely: these may be weak or unstable. • Constituencies: the link between the voter and their representative is weaker as the constituencies are so large and have several different representatives. • Complex counting system. • Complex voting process: voters may find it difficult or confusing if they lack the knowledge to choose between different parties *and* candidates.	• Does not deliver a fully proportional result, as the majority of the seats are FPTP. • Two classes of representative are elected: some represent constituencies, others larger regions. • Voters cannot choose between individual candidates on the closed list, just between parties. • Majority governments are less likely than with FPTP. • Relatively complex voting system: the voter makes two choices and needs to understand two voting systems.

Typical mistake

Don't assume that any alternative to FPTP will benefit minor parties: this is not the case. Proportional systems will increase the representation of smaller parties, but majoritarian systems will not. This is because minor parties find it difficult to win a majority of the vote unless their supporters are geographically concentrated (as in the case of the Scottish National Party).

Impact of electoral systems on the party system

REVISED

- FPTP tends to produce a two-party system, with a single party forming a majority government.
- In recent years, voters' growing support for minor and regional parties has led to a coalition and a minority government.
- This has resulted in suggestions that the UK is now in effect a multi-party system that would benefit from a different electoral system.

- Majoritarian systems such as SV tend to produce a two-party system. They make it harder for more extreme minor parties to win seats than under FPTP, as they need a majority of votes. It is easier for centrist minor parties (e.g. the Liberal Democrats) to win seats, as they are more likely to be a second preference.
- Proportional systems such as STV usually result in a multi-party system, with coalition governments.
- The mixed system AMS has allowed a multi-party system to emerge in Scotland, but one in which larger parties enjoy a winner's bonus from seats elected using FPTP. Coalition or minority governments are the most likely outcome of a Scottish Parliament election, but it is still possible for a party to form a majority government: the SNP did so in 2011.

Now test yourself

TESTED

5 What is a majoritarian system?
6 What type of system is the STV?
7 Where is the SV system used in the UK?
8 What impact do proportional systems have on the party system?

Answers on p. 111

Exam tip

It can be difficult to remember all the different voting systems: the best way is to develop your own opinion about which systems are best for democracy. This will also help you to analyse the electoral systems in the exam.

Revision activity

1 Write down as many advantages and disadvantages of the following as you can from memory:
   - FPTP
   - majoritarian systems
   - proportional systems
2 Check your answers against the information in this section and add in any missing points.
3 Decide which are the strongest and weakest arguments in favour of each voting system.

Exam tip

Students often waste too much time explaining *how* the different voting systems work, rather than analysing their *impact*. As a general rule, avoid writing more than a sentence of explanation for each system.

Voting behaviour

Voting behaviour describes how people tend to vote. The study of voting behaviour includes looking at patterns of *how* people vote and analysis of *why* they vote that way.

Factors influencing voting behaviour

REVISED

Age

- In 2017 age was the most important predictor of how people voted in the general election.
- Young people were more likely to vote Labour than older people (over the age of 47), who were more likely to vote Conservative.
- In the 2016 EU referendum, a majority of 18- to 34-year-olds voted to remain, whereas a majority of over-55s voted to leave.
- Turnout increases with age: 57% of 18- and 19-year-olds voted in the 2017 general election, compared to 84% of those aged 70 years or more.

Class

- Traditionally, class was the main predictor of how people would vote: working-class voters were more likely to support Labour, whereas middle-class voters were more likely to support the Conservatives.
- Since the 1980s, the process of class dealignment has meant that class is less important in determining voting behaviour.
- Middle-class voters were more likely to vote to remain in the 2016 EU referendum than working-class voters of the same age.

Gender

- Men and women may have different priorities: some believe that women are more likely to support parties that favour strong public services, particularly the NHS and education.
- Women were more likely to vote to remain in the EU than men.
- Women are as likely to turn out to vote as men.

Ethnicity

- Black, Asian and minority ethnic (BAME) groups are significantly more likely to vote Labour than Conservative.
- White voters are more likely to vote Conservative than Labour.

Geography

- Rural English areas and southern constituencies are more likely to be Conservative.
- Urban areas, particularly in London and the North, are more likely to be held by Labour, as is much of south Wales.
- Regional parties dominate in Scotland and Northern Ireland and have an important presence in Wales.

> **Typical mistake**
>
> Don't assume that class is the most important factor in determining voting behaviour; this is no longer true. Age and geography are much more reliable predictors of how people vote.

Voter choice

REVISED

A number of theories of voter choice are given in Table 7.3.

Table 7.3 Theories of voter choice

Theory	Key features
Rational choice theory	Assumes that voters weigh up all the political options logically and vote for the party that will deliver the best result for them.
Issue voting	Voters prioritise one issue above all others and vote purely based on that issue.
Valence issues	Valence issues are those that are universally accepted to be important. Voters choose a party based on how well they think the party will perform on those issues. The economy is probably the most important valence issue. Other valence issues include healthcare and education.

> **Typical mistake**
>
> Don't confuse issue voting and rational choice voting. People may be so committed to a single issue that they vote *against* their own best interests. For example, imagine a business owner who exported goods to the EU but who prioritised reducing immigration above all else. They might well have voted Leave in the 2016 EU referendum, despite the likely negative impact on their business.

Now test yourself

TESTED

9 Which factor was traditionally most important in explaining voting behaviour?

10 Which factor was the most important predictor of voting behaviour in the 2017 general election?

11 Which party are BAME groups most likely to support?

12 In which geographical regions do the Conservatives dominate most?

Answers on p. 111

Election case studies

7 Elections and referendums

Case study: The 1979 general election

Table 7.4 **The 1979 general election**

Political context	• Followed the 1978–79 'Winter of Discontent' strikes • Labour leader James Callaghan faced new Conservative leader Margaret Thatcher
Result	• Conservative win • 43-seat majority
Patterns of voting behaviour	• Middle class more likely to vote Conservative, working class more likely to vote Labour • All ages more likely to vote Conservative, apart from 18- to 24-year-olds • Women slightly more likely to vote Conservative than Labour, men equally likely • No records for BAME voters
Influence of the media	• More media focus on leaders than previously • Thatcher used television photo opportunities to raise her profile • The *Sun* newspaper switched support from Labour to the Conservatives for the first time
Impact of party policies	• The Conservatives focused on getting the economy going again, lowering unemployment and preventing strike disruption
Influence of manifestos	• Conservative tax cuts and the Right to Buy scheme (giving council tenants the right to buy their council house at a heavily discounted price) were popular with voters
Impact of campaigns and leadership	• Successful 'Labour isn't working' **campaign** by Conservatives focused on high unemployment • Thatcher was relatively unknown compared to Callaghan. Some voters found her manner off-putting • British voters had no model for what a female prime minister would look and sound like
Impact of elections on policy and policy making	• Thatcher's majority allowed her to begin transforming Britain by privatising public industries, reducing union strikes and adopting a **monetarist economic policy** (which led to unemployment doubling by 1983) • Thatcher's policies became even bolder after she won a landslide in 1983

Campaign An attempt by a political party to persuade people to vote for its candidates or, in the case of a referendum, in accordance with its views.

Monetarist economic policy Economic policy that aims to keep inflation low by controlling the supply of money.

AQA AS/A-level Politics: UK politics 65

Case study: The 1997 general election

Table 7.5 The 1997 general election

Political context	<ul><li>The Conservatives had been in power since 1979 and prime minister John Major's government was tainted by sleaze (financial and sex scandals)</li><li>Labour had moved to the centre politically since Tony Blair became leader in 1994</li></ul>
Result	<ul><li>Labour landslide</li><li>179-seat majority</li><li>Best postwar result of any party</li><li>Best result ever for Labour</li></ul>
Patterns of voting behaviour	<ul><li>Labour made big gains among the middle class and skilled working class</li><li>All ages more likely to vote Labour, apart from the over-65s</li><li>Women and men equally likely to support Labour</li><li>70% of BAME voters supported Labour, compared to 43% of white voters</li></ul>
Influence of the media	<ul><li>**New Labour** had a proactive approach to the media that was new to UK politics</li><li>Tony Blair went to Australia after becoming leader to meet Rupert Murdoch, owner of the *Sun* newspaper</li><li>The *Sun* switched support from the Conservatives to Labour</li><li>'**Spin doctors**' managed Labour's interactions with the media to ensure that daily stories kept coverage 'on message'</li></ul>
Impact of party policies	<ul><li>Labour had centrist economic policies</li><li>The **third way** was designed to appeal to a broad range of voters</li><li>The Conservatives were divided over Europe and very critical of Blair's devolution plans, neither of which impressed the electorate</li></ul>
Influence of manifestos	<ul><li>Labour made five pledges: to cut classroom sizes, to introduce fast-track punishments for persistent young offenders, to cut NHS waiting lists, to get under-25-year-olds into work and not to raise income tax</li></ul>
Impact of campaigns and leadership	<ul><li>Negative campaigning from the Conservatives, with 'New Labour, New Danger' slogan</li><li>The Labour slogan promised change: 'Because Britain deserves better'</li><li>Campaigns focused on party leaders</li><li>At 43, Blair was younger than any prime minister since 1812 and lacked experience. However, his charisma and enthusiasm appealed to voters, as did his amendment in 1995 of **Clause IV** of Labour's constitution</li></ul>
Impact of elections on policy and policy making	<ul><li>Blair's huge majority allowed him to implement a wide range of policies including devolution, the removal of hereditary peers from the House of Lords, the passing of the Human Rights Act 1998 and the Freedom of Information Act 2000, the introduction of a national minimum wage and increased public spending</li></ul>

New Labour The policies and values introduced by Tony Blair after he became leader in 1994, which dominated until Ed Miliband became leader in 2010. New Labour accepted the capitalist economic system and focused on equality of opportunity rather than equality of outcome (giving people equal opportunities, but not an equal standard of living). New Labour was a 'catch-all' party with broad appeal to different social classes, including the middle class.

'Spin doctors' Political operatives who shape a politician's message so that it attracts maximum positive publicity. Blair's New Labour was famous for its use of spin doctors: the best-known were Alastair Campbell and Peter Mandelson.

Third way An ideological compromise developed by Blair's New Labour. It was a balance between centre-right economic policy and centre-left social policy, which focused on social justice rather than a socialist restructuring of the economic system.

Clause IV Part of the 1918 Labour constitution, which committed Labour to the 'common ownership of the means of production, distribution and exchange', meaning widespread nationalisation. In 1995 Blair rewrote the clause, removing references to socialist economic policy.

Case study: The 2017 general election

Table 7.6 The 2017 general election

Political context	• The election was not due until 2020, but prime minister Theresa May called a **snap election**, hoping to win a mandate for her Brexit policies • Labour leader Jeremy Corbyn's poll ratings were very low: May assumed she would win a large majority
Result	• Hung parliament • A Conservative minority government dependent on a confidence and supply deal (see p. 30) with the Democratic Unionist Party (DUP) • The Conservatives lost 13 seats, Labour gained 30
Patterns of voting behaviour	• In 2017, 46% of social grade AB (typically households with the highest incomes, usually professional or managerial) voted Conservative and 38% Labour, whereas 41% of social grade DE (typically households with the lowest incomes, including unskilled workers and unemployed) voted Conservative and 44% Labour • Age was the key predictor of voting behaviour: the younger a voter, the more likely they were to vote Labour • In 2017, women supported Labour and the Conservatives equally, whereas 39% of men voted Labour and 45% Conservative • In 2017, 73% of BAME voters supported Labour and 19% Conservative • Described as the return of two-party politics because the Conservatives' and Labour's combined share of the vote exceeded 80%, the first time this had happened since the 1980s. This was mainly due to the collapse of the UKIP vote from 3.9 million in 2015 to just 590,000 in 2017
Influence of the media	• Jeremy Corbyn's policies, personality and leadership style were widely criticised by the media • Many newspapers, including the *Sun*, supported the Conservatives • May was weakened by her refusal to participate in the televised leaders' debates • Labour used social media to counter its negative publicity from traditional media and to reach out to younger people
Impact of party policies	• The Conservatives' focus on Brexit was uninspiring • Labour wanted to spend more on public services • May's plans to reduce spending on pensions gave the impression that the Conservatives were abandoning their most loyal supporters: the elderly
Influence of manifestos	• The Conservative manifesto seemed ill-considered and senior Conservatives complained they had not been consulted • May's attempt to improve inter-generational fairness by making people pay for home care if they had assets of more than £100,000 was labelled the 'dementia tax'. She was forced to modify her plans • Labour's promise to abolish university tuition fees appealed to younger voters
Impact of campaigns and leadership	• May began the campaign with a huge lead over Corbyn in the polls, but was far less popular than him by election day • May's refusal to participate in televised debates and her aloof personal style were partly responsible • The Conservative campaign was based on May's abilities as a leader, promising 'strong and stable' government: this backfired when her personality and policies failed to connect with voters
Impact of elections on policy and policy making	• May lost her majority but won the most seats, so formed a government with the help of the DUP • May's leadership was fundamentally weakened • The Conservatives were unable to deliver many manifesto commitments • May was forced to negotiate Brexit while dependent on her highly critical and divided MPs

Snap election A general election that is held earlier than expected and typically occurs relatively quickly after being announced. A government may seek a snap election if it believes it can win a big majority. The Fixed-term Parliaments Act 2011 states that general elections should happen every five years, but a government can still trigger a snap election if at least two-thirds of MPs vote for it.

Typical mistake

Don't exaggerate Labour's success in the 2017 election. Although the party increased its share of the vote and prevented Theresa May from winning a majority, the Conservatives also increased their share of the vote (because voters switched from UKIP) and *won* the election (albeit without a majority).

Exam tip

The best answers use examples to support their analysis, so learn the details of these case studies and try to apply them to different questions on elections. You may also be asked to refer specifically to case studies, depending on the question. You are expected to understand one election before 1997, the 1997 general election itself and one election after 1997.

Revision activity

Using the three case studies given here, make a list of the main factors that influenced the outcome of each election.

Examples of particular characteristics of the British electoral system

REVISED

Table 7.7 characterises a selection of British general elections.

Disenfranchised Someone's right to vote has been removed.

Table 7.7 Examples of characteristics of British general elections

A landslide victory for one party	**1997 (Labour)** ● The biggest landslide victory since the Second World War.
A clear discrepancy between the number of votes and the number of seats gained	**2015 (Conservative)** ● UKIP won 3.9 million votes but gained just one seat in the House of Commons. ● The Greens won 1.1 million votes and also won one seat. ● The contrast between UKIP and the SNP's result was even more startling: the SNP was rewarded with 56 MPs for just 1.5 million votes.
Large numbers of voters being effectively **disenfranchised** by the preponderance of voters for one party in large areas of the country	**2015 (Conservative)** ● The SNP won a landslide victory in Scotland, winning 56 of 59 seats. For the first time in its history, it became the third largest party in the UK Parliament. ● 1.5 million Scots voted for the SNP, nearly 50% of the popular vote. ● This means that just over 50% of the Scottish popular vote went *against* the SNP, yet it received 95% of Scottish seats in the House of Commons. ● Scottish voters who did not support the SNP might claim to be effectively disenfranchised as their votes did not translate into representation in the Commons.
An election in which the outcome was greatly influenced by a particular leadership style or personality	**1997 (Labour)** ● Blair's leadership was crucial to Labour's landslide win. ● He was young, charismatic and a skilled communicator. He used 'spin doctors' to manipulate the media and convinced Rupert Murdoch of the *Sun* to support him. ● He had the vision and leadership to create New Labour, moving the party into the centre of the political spectrum and reassuring many middle-class voters that Labour could be trusted with the economy. **2017 (Conservative)** ● Having chosen to fight an election based on her own leadership abilities, May failed to connect with voters. ● A combination of political mistakes, May's personal style and her refusal to appear in the televised debates resulted in her losing her majority.

Exam tip

You need to have examples for the different scenarios listed in Table 7.7, so make sure you learn these examples.

Referendums

Referendum rules and procedures

REVISED ☐

- There is no legal requirement for most referendums to be held. However, the Government of Wales Act 2006 required a referendum for further changes to Welsh devolution (this happened in 2011) and the Scotland Act 2016 forbids the abolition of the Scottish Parliament without a referendum.

- It has become a constitutional convention that referendums will be called for significant constitutional change, such as the referendums on AV (2011), Scottish independence (2014) and membership of the EU (2016).

- The government can set any referendum question, but the Electoral Commission comments on proposed questions. The government is likely to take their advice.

- Any group or individual spending over £10,000 has to register with the Electoral Commission and is given spending limits.

- The Electoral Commission oversees the conduct of the referendum and writes a report afterwards.

- The result of the referendum is not legally binding. Parliament is still sovereign, so the government can ignore the result in theory, although in practice this would be profoundly undemocratic.

A number of reasons for calling referendums are given in Table 7.8.

Table 7.8 Reasons for calling referendums

Reason	Significance
Constitutional change	To give a specific mandate for planned constitutional change, e.g. in 1997 the devolution of Scotland and Wales.
Political forces	Governments may feel compelled to call a referendum if nationalist parties are gaining ground, e.g. the 2014 Scottish independence referendum and the 2016 EU referendum.
Party or government management	To settle an issue: prime ministers may hold a referendum on an issue that is dividing their party or government. This happened in 1975 when the Labour government was divided over remaining in the EEC and in 2011 when the Conservative–Liberal Democrat coalition government held a referendum on changing the voting system, which the Liberal Democrats supported but not the Conservatives.
The Localism Act 2011	This Act was intended to devolve power to local governments, including an increase in local referendums. Local referendums must be called on certain plans for housing development and to increase council tax above levels set by central government. By October 2016, 52 referendums had been held to decide if directly elected mayors should be introduced (16 voted 'yes').

UK referendums

Table 7.9 outlines the main referendums held in the UK since 1975.

Table 7.9 UK referendums since 1975

Referendum	Context	Result	Impact
UK European Communities membership referendum, 1975	Labour prime minister Harold Wilson called this referendum because his party and cabinet were split over Europe	67% of the electorate voted to stay in the EEC	Britain remained in the EEC, which later developed into the European Union (EU)
Scottish devolution referendum, 1979 Welsh devolution referendum, 1979	Growing calls for devolution	Scotland voted to have their own assembly (parliament), but did not meet the 40% **threshold** set by the government Wales voted against an assembly	Devolution did not happen Scottish nationalists were hugely frustrated that the vote did not meet the threshold
Scottish devolution referendum, 1997 Welsh devolution referendum, 1997	Tony Blair used referendums to legitimise his constitutional changes He introduced a Scottish Parliament and a Welsh Assembly	Scotland voted 'yes' by 74% to 25% In Wales the result was more ambiguous: with only a 50% turnout, 50.3% voted 'yes' to 49.7% 'no'	The Scottish Parliament and Welsh Assembly were set up Each was given devolved powers
Greater London Authority referendum, 1998	Part of Blair's devolution programme	A clear majority voted yes (72%) A low turnout of 34% was a poor mandate for local devolution	London gained its own assembly and a directly elected mayor
Northern Ireland Good Friday Agreement referendum, 1998	A landmark moment in UK history People of Northern Ireland were asked to support the peace agreement that aimed to end 'the Troubles' (see p. 46)	71% of voters supported the agreement A high turnout of 81% gave the agreement crucial legitimacy	A devolved assembly was set up A 'power sharing' agreement gave republicans and unionists a role in government STV was used for assembly elections, ensuring the sensitive mix of political opinion in Northern Ireland was accurately reflected
North East England devolution referendum, 2004	Blair's Labour government planned to extend devolution to the regions of the UK by introducing regional assemblies, starting with the northeast of England	78% of voters in the northeast rejected the plan A low turnout of 48% also suggested that this referendum had not sparked much public interest	The government was surprised and disappointed This referendum effectively ended government plans to introduce regional devolution
Welsh devolution referendum, 2011	Plaid Cymru and Welsh Labour both wanted to increase Wales's law-making powers	Wales voted 'yes' (63%) A very low turnout of 35.6%	Wales received greater law-making powers

Referendum	Context	Result	Impact
UK Alternative Vote referendum, 2011	The coalition agreement included a referendum on AV as a compromise: the Conservatives wanted to keep FPTP, whereas the Lib Dems wanted proportional representation (PR) The public struggled to understand the complexities of the AV system and the campaigns failed to inspire	68% voted to keep FPTP Only 42% of the electorate turned out	FPTP continues to be used for UK general elections The low turnout and emphatic rejection of AV makes it unlikely that any political party will attempt to change the voting system again for many years
Scottish independence referendum, 2014	Prime minister David Cameron was criticised by some Conservatives for calling this referendum as it risked the break-up of the UK Cameron argued that he had no choice: the SNP had won a majority in the 2011 Scottish Parliament elections with an independence referendum in their manifesto The SNP campaigned for 'Yes Scotland' while the Tories, Lib Dems and Labour ran 'Better together'	55% of voters chose to remain in the UK There was a record turnout of 84.5% The campaigns saw huge political participation across Scotland 16- and 17-year-olds were allowed to vote	Scotland remained in the UK Following the 2016 EU referendum (in which Scotland voted to remain), the Scottish government, led by SNP leader Nicola Sturgeon, pushed for a second Scottish independence referendum After losing seats in the 2017 election, Sturgeon decided to wait until Brexit was finished, as her focus on a second referendum had contributed to the poor result
UK European Union membership referendum, 2016	In their 2015 manifesto, the Conservatives promised an EU referendum Cameron included the referendum to stop Tory voters from switching to UKIP and to placate **eurosceptics** in his party The campaigns were cross-party. Tories Boris Johnson and Michael Gove headed the Vote Leave campaign with Labour MP Gisela Stuart. UKIP ran a separate Leave campaign Cameron and most government ministers campaigned for Remain, along with much of Labour and all Liberal Democrats The Leave campaigns were criticised for inaccurate claims, while Remain focused on economic risks and failed to give positive reasons to stay	52% voted to leave, 48% to remain Turnout was high, at 72%	Cameron resigned: he had taken a massive political gamble, but it had failed Theresa May became prime minister, aiming to lead Britain through the Brexit process The British public seemed divided as never before The decision to leave put parliament (where a majority wished to remain) at odds with a majority of the people. However, most MPs felt that they had a duty to carry out the wishes of the electorate In February 2017 MPs voted to allow the process of leaving the European Union

> **Threshold** The minimum proportion of the electorate who need to vote 'yes' in a referendum in order for their decision to be implemented. The government decides whether to set a threshold. A threshold is not generally used in the UK, but the most notable exception was the 1979 Scottish devolution referendum.
>
> **Eurosceptics** Those who do not support the increasing powers of the EU and are suspicious and critical of it.

Impact of referendums on democracy

REVISED

Table 7.10 gives a number of positive and negative impacts of referendums on democracy.

Table 7.10 Positive and negative impacts of referendums

Positive	Negative
<ul><li>Referendums have enhanced direct democracy, telling politicians what the electorate think more accurately than any opinion poll.</li><li>High turnout in some referendums is evidence of improved political participation.</li><li>Referendums give legitimacy to important decisions.</li><li>The regular use of referendums since 1998 suggests that they have been an effective means of decision making.</li><li>The electorate has surprised the government on several occasions, causing shifts in policy that would otherwise not have happened.</li></ul>	<ul><li>Governments still hold the power, not the people: governments tend not to hold referendums that they think they might lose.</li><li>Low turnout in some referendums suggests that the public are not always engaged.</li><li>Referendums threaten parliamentary sovereignty and representative democracy.</li><li>Poor-quality campaigns can mislead or confuse the public.</li><li>Referendums offer no protection against the tyranny of the majority (when the majority of people may vote for something that undermines the rights of a minority group).</li></ul>

Exam tip

If you are asked about the impact of referendums, make sure you use specific, recent examples. This tells the examiner that you are fully up to date. They would think it strange if you did not mention the 2016 EU referendum at all.

Revision activity

Make a list of different types of referendums, adding all the referendums in Table 7.9 as examples:
- national referendums
- devolved nations only (Scotland, Wales and Northern Ireland)
- regional referendums
- local referendums

Now test yourself

TESTED

17 How many national referendums have there been?
18 In which circumstance has calling a referendum become a convention?
19 Which referendum in the UK had the highest turnout?
20 Why did the 2016 EU referendum challenge parliamentary sovereignty?

Answers on p. 111

Summary

You should now have an understanding of:
- the FPTP electoral system and its advantages and disadvantages
- majoritarian and proportional electoral systems, their advantages and disadvantages and their impact on the party system
- the factors influencing voting behaviour
- three general election case studies — 1979, 1997 and 2017 – and patterns of voting behaviour in those elections
- the influence and impact of the media, party policies, manifestos, campaigns and leadership in the three election case studies, and their impact on policy and policy making
- examples of particular characteristics of British elections
- the nature and use of referendums in the UK and their impact

Exam practice

AS

1 Explain, with examples, the use of proportional electoral systems.

[6]

A-level

2 Explain and analyse three features of the FPTP voting system.

[9]

3 'The use of referendums since 1998 has strengthened UK democracy.' Analyse and evaluate this statement.

[25]

4 'Party leadership is the most important factor in determining the outcome of UK general elections.' Analyse and evaluate this statement, with reference to one pre-1997 election, the 1997 election and one post-1997 election.

[25]

Answers and quick quiz 7 online

ONLINE

8 Political parties

Key points

- The UK has a wide variety of political parties, with a diverse range of ideas and policies.
- The extent to which ordinary members are able to participate in decision making varies between the Conservatives, Labour and the Liberal Democrats.
- Party funding is a controversial issue, particularly given the impact of wealthy donors.
- Political parties win elections because of many different factors, one of which is their relationship with the media.
- Minor parties play an increasingly important role in UK politics, leading some to argue that the UK now has a multi-party system.

Origins, ideas and development

Conservatives

Table 8.1 outlines the origins, ideas and development of the Conservative Party.

Table 8.1 The Conservative Party

Origins	• Dates back to 1834. • Traditionally the party represented the wealthy. • Once universal suffrage was introduced in Britain in 1928, the party reinvented itself to appeal to a broader range of supporters. • Benjamin Disraeli (leader 1868–81) developed **one-nation conservatism** to attract support from new working-class voters. • Dominated UK politics in the twentieth century, with 67 years in office.
Ideas	• One-nation conservatism dominated before 1979. • **Thatcherism** was a much more radical, **neo-liberal** version of conservatism. It was part of the New Right movement that included US president Ronald Reagan. • 'Compassionate conservatism' was adopted by David Cameron: it combined Thatcherite free-market economic policies with more liberal social policies (e.g. gay marriage) and concern for the welfare of both society and the environment. • Austerity was the key feature of Cameron's governments. The 2008 financial crisis left Britain with a massive deficit and a growing national debt: the Conservatives responded by cutting public spending. • There have been many battles between eurosceptics and **europhiles**: even after the 2016 vote to leave the EU, debates continue between Brexiteers and Remainers.
Development	• Conservatives accepted the **postwar consensus** before Margaret Thatcher became leader. • Thatcher (leader 1975–90) was impatient with her party's tolerance of high taxation, powerful and disruptive unions and economic stagnation. • Thatcher moved the UK sharply to the right when she became prime minister in 1979. • Thatcher adopted a confident foreign policy: protecting one of the UK's overseas territories in the 1982 Falklands War, playing a leading role alongside Ronald Reagan in Cold War diplomacy and winning a financial rebate from the European Community (which later became the EU).

Development	• Thatcher's successor as prime minister, John Major, largely continued Thatcherite policies. The struggles within the party over Europe intensified during his leadership.
	• The party passed through a period in the political wilderness during the New Labour era.
	• David Cameron aimed to detoxify the Conservative Party's 'nasty party' image when he became leader in 2005.
	• The Conservatives won most seats in 2010 and formed a coalition with the Liberal Democrats. In 2015 Cameron won a small majority.
	• Cameron's decision to hold a referendum on Britain's EU membership was a big mistake: he resigned as prime minister after failing to convince the public to remain.
	• Theresa May signalled that she wished to follow one-nation policies when she became leader, but her 2017 manifesto's support of grammar schools, fox hunting and the removal of universal free school lunches for 4- to 7-year-olds suggested a move away from Cameron's modern conservatism.
	• May's failed attempt to win a big majority in 2017 by calling a snap election left her leading a minority government, dependent on the Democratic Unionist Party (DUP) for votes and unable to develop her own version of conservatism.
	• The Conservatives were divided during the Brexit process, forcing May to balance Brexiteers and Remainers carefully in her government.

One-nation conservatism A version of conservatism that includes policies designed to benefit all sections of society.

Thatcherism Margaret Thatcher's distinctive brand of conservatism. It included a monetarist economic policy (see p. 65), deregulation of business and finance, privatisation of industry and restriction of trade union powers.

Neo-liberal A liberal ideology that promotes free-market capitalism.

Europhiles Those who support the EU project and see the EU as a force for good.

Postwar consensus The acceptance by both of the main political parties that Britain should retain the postwar settlement (the nationalised industries and generous welfare state first introduced by the 1945 Labour government).

Typical mistake

Remember that not all Conservatives oppose change: Thatcher introduced sweeping changes to Britain. However, her reforms had a conservative basis as her aim was to return Britain to its former glory.

Labour

REVISED

Table 8.2 outlines the origins, ideas and development of the Labour Party.

Table 8.2 The Labour Party

Origins	• The Labour Representation Committee was formed in 1900.
	• It included trade unions and left-wing political groups.
	• The aim was to represent the working class in parliament.
	• Labour rejected **revolutionary socialism**, focusing instead on social democracy.
	• The party's 1918 constitution committed Labour to socialism.
	• Labour formed its first government in 1929 but did not win a majority until 1945.
	• The 1945 Labour government created the NHS and the welfare state and nationalised many industries. These reforms formed the basis of the postwar consensus.
Ideas	• Socialism is an ideology aiming for equality between people, through common ownership of the means of production (public ownership of factories and industries) and redistribution of wealth from rich to poor.
	• Social democracy is the democratic version of socialism. Socialists win power within a democratic (usually capitalist) system, and introduce changes, e.g. nationalisation, high taxation, a welfare state.

Ideas	• Clause IV is part of the 1918 constitution; it committed Labour to the 'common ownership of the means of production, distribution and exchange', meaning widespread nationalisation. • The third way is an ideological compromise developed by New Labour. It balanced centre-right economic policy and centre-left social policy. • Corbynism is described by many as a return to **Old Labour**. It advocates the renationalisation of the railways and utilities, reversing austerity and increasing taxes on business to pay for the welfare state.
Development	• Labour moved to the left after its 1979 defeat by Thatcher. It struggled electorally. • In 1994 Tony Blair became leader. He recognised the economic successes of Thatcherism and aimed to **triangulate** Labour's policies. With his ally Gordon Brown, he launched New Labour, which adopted the third way. • In 1995 Blair rewrote Clause IV, removing references to socialist economic policy. This reassured middle-class potential voters. • In 1997 Labour won a landslide victory. It implemented devolution, the removal of hereditary peers from the House of Lords, the passing of the Human Rights Act 1998 and the Freedom of Information Act 2000, the introduction of a national minimum wage and increased public spending. • Blair's reputation never recovered from his decision to commit Britain to the war in Iraq in 2003 (see p. 35). • When Blair stood down in 2007, Gordon Brown served as prime minister until his defeat in the 2010 election. Brown had nurtured Labour's economic reputation as chancellor of the exchequer, but this was weakened by the impact of the 2008 global financial crisis. • New leader Ed Miliband defeated one of New Labour's best-known figures, his own elder brother, in the leadership contest. Miliband moved the party slightly to the left and was vilified by right-wing newspapers. • Miliband failed to win over the electorate: the party was defeated in the 2015 election. • Blairites called for a return to centrist policies but the party elected Jeremy Corbyn as leader in 2015. • Corbyn represented a dramatic break with New Labour: he was the most rebellious backbencher during Blair's government and led the Stop the War coalition against the war in Iraq. He is also opposed to nuclear weapons. He is backed by the grassroots movement Momentum. • Despite media criticism of Corbyn, Labour's share of the vote increased in 2017, although they remained second to the Conservatives.

Revolutionary socialism An ideology that aims to create a socialist society through revolution.

Old Labour The traditional policies and values of the Labour Party. These include a commitment to socialism, nationalisation, the welfare state, high taxation and the redistribution of wealth.

Triangulation Tony Blair's repositioning of Labour on the political spectrum, moving towards Thatcherism on economic policy, but retaining traditional Labour social values.

Liberal Democrats

REVISED

Table 8.3 outlines the origins, ideas and development of the Liberal Democrat Party.

Table 8.3 The Liberal Democrat Party

Origins	<ul><li>Formed from two different parties: the Liberal Party and the Social Democratic Party (SDP).</li><li>The Liberal Party was once one of the two main parties in UK politics, but after the First World War it was pushed into third place by the Labour Party.</li><li>The SDP was formed in 1981, when four leading Labour politicians (the 'gang of four') left Labour in protest at its increasingly left-wing policies.</li><li>In 1981 the SDP formed an electoral pact with the Liberal Party, known as 'The Alliance'.</li><li>In 1988 the two parties merged to form the Liberal Democrats.</li></ul>
Ideas	<ul><li>Liberalism is an ideology based on freedom. This includes individual freedom and free trade.</li><li>Social democracy is the democratic version of socialism. Socialists win power within a democratic (usually capitalist) system, and introduce changes, e.g. nationalisation, high taxation, a welfare state.</li><li>Social liberalism is focused on a liberal form of social democracy. Social liberals are keen to dismantle Thatcher's economic policies and to redistribute wealth via higher taxation on the wealthy. Many were once members of the SDP and the Labour Party prior to that.</li><li>'Orange Book' liberalism is so-called because of a book written by prominent liberals, *The Orange Book: Reclaiming Liberalism*. These thinkers accepted the free market and did not significantly challenge Thatcherite economic policies.</li><li>Electoral reform is a top priority for Liberal Democrats. The Alliance famously won 26% of the vote in 1983 but only 23 seats in the House of Commons. The party argues for a proportional electoral system.</li><li>Unlike Labour and the Conservatives, the Liberal Democrats have been consistently enthusiastic about the EU.</li></ul>
Development	<ul><li>Tony Blair considered forming a coalition with the Liberal Democrats, but his large majority in 1997 meant this was not necessary.</li><li>The Liberal Democrats won 46 seats in 1997 with leader Paddy Ashdown. His successor, Charles Kennedy, oversaw the party's best result of 62 seats in 2005. This was partly a result of the party's opposition to the Iraq War.</li><li>Nick Clegg became leader in 2007. He was from the centre-right of the party and had contributed to *The Orange Book*.</li><li>Clegg was ideally placed to join forces with David Cameron when the Conservatives failed to win a majority in 2010. Both men were towards the centre of the political spectrum: Clegg was towards the right of his party and Cameron was towards the left of his.</li><li>From 2010 to 2015, the Liberal Democrats had their first experience of government, in coalition with the Conservatives. Nick Clegg became deputy prime minister.</li><li>As part of the coalition agreement, the Liberal Democrats agreed to increase university tuition fees. Their signature pledge had been not to raise fees, so they were seen as having broken a promise and abandoned students, some of their core voters.</li><li>The coalition meant the Liberal Democrats were associated with economic austerity and reduced public spending. This alienated many of their more left-wing supporters. The coalition erased the Liberal Democrats' unique identity: many voters were left wondering what the difference was between them and the Conservatives.</li><li>The year 2015 was a disastrous election for the Liberal Democrats: their numbers were cut to just 8 MPs. Nick Clegg resigned as leader.</li><li>The Liberal Democrats campaigned hard for Remain during the 2016 EU referendum, but were unsuccessful.</li><li>The party hoped to attract angry Remainers in the 2017 election, but won only 14 seats.</li></ul>

Typical mistake

Remember that the Liberal Democrats stopped being the third largest UK party in the House of Commons in 2015, when they were overtaken by the SNP.

Current policies

The three main parties

REVISED

The current policies of the three main parties in the UK are given in Table 8.4.

Table 8.4 Current policies of the main political parties

2017 election manifesto	Conservatives	Labour	Liberal Democrats
Economy	Continue working towards a balanced budget	Nationalisation of railways and energy, water and Royal Mail More borrowing than the Conservatives	Infrastructure investment More borrowing than the Conservatives
Health	£8 billion in extra funding over 5 years	£30 billion in extra funding over 5 years	£6 billion per year for the NHS and social care
Education	Increase the number of good school places and develop a knowledge-rich curriculum	Abolish university tuition fees. Establish a National Education Service for lifelong learning	Increase education funding and funding for the poorest students
Tax	Raise thresholds of personal tax allowance (the level at which income starts to be taxed) Cut corporation tax	High earners and big corporations to pay more tax	1% rise on income tax, to raise £6 billion per year. This money to be ring-fenced for the NHS and social care
Defence	Renew the **Trident nuclear deterrent** Spend at least 2% of gross domestic product (GDP) on defence, in line with the **North Atlantic Treaty Organization (NATO)** target	Renew the Trident nuclear deterrent Meet NATO target of 2% of GDP defence spending	Downgrade the UK's nuclear deterrent to a less costly version Campaign for international nuclear disarmament Meet NATO target of 2% of GDP defence spending
The environment	Improve air quality Support fracking (a way of extracting natural gas from underground, which can damage the environment)	Ban fracking Move to a low-carbon economy	Ban fracking Improve air quality, oppose Heathrow airport expansion and introduce a diesel scrappage scheme
Brexit	No deal with the EU is better than a bad deal for the UK	Make a viable deal with the EU involving a new UK-EU customs union	Promise to hold a second referendum

Trident nuclear deterrent Britain's continuous at-sea nuclear deterrent, which has been in operation since 1969. The UK has four nuclear submarines, one of which is always at sea. Even if all of Britain's land-based defences were destroyed, the Trident nuclear missiles could still be fired from sea.

North Atlantic Treaty Organization (NATO) An international organisation of 29 Western nations including the UK, the USA, Germany, France and Turkey. Members agree to collectively protect each other's security: an aggressive attack on one NATO member is considered an act upon all.

Typical mistake

Don't argue that the main political parties have moved closer together on the political spectrum. Although this was perhaps true for Blair's Labour Party and Cameron's Conservative Party, it has not been true in the May/Corbyn era. Labour has moved to the left under Corbyn and since the 2016 EU referendum the Conservatives have moved to the right.

Revision activity

Using Table 8.4, find examples of policies that link to the following ideologies:
- one-nation conservatism
- Thatcherism
- socialism
- social liberalism

Party structures and functions

Participation

REVISED

Figure 8.1 gives an overview of participation within a political party.

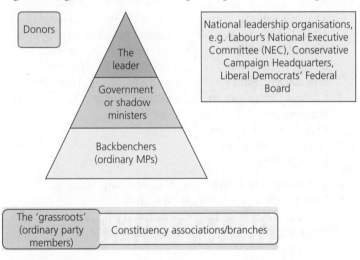

Figure 8.1 **Who participates within a political party?**

Functions

REVISED

- Representation: parties represent the ideology and views of their members.
- Participation: parties provide opportunities for people to participate in politics.
- Recruitment: parties recruit and select candidates for elections.
- Policy: parties develop policies and offer these to the electorate in their manifestos.
- Government: parties provide voters with a clear choice of different governments. Once elected, the party helps to organise and discipline MPs to support the government's **political agenda**.

Political agenda The political issues that are prioritised by political parties, the media or in general public debate.

Structure and membership

The structure and membership of the three main parties in the UK are given in Table 8.5.

Table 8.5 Structure and membership of the main political parties

	Conservatives	Labour	Liberal Democrats
Local and national structure	• Each constituency has a Conservative Association; these help run election campaigns. • There is a Welsh Conservative Party and a Scottish Conservative Party within the UK Conservative Party. • The National Conservative Convention makes decisions for the voluntary party. Constituency association chairs attend, as do regional officers and representatives from the party's youth and women's organisations. • The 1922 Committee is made up of backbench Conservative MPs. • Conservative Campaign Headquarters (CCHQ) is the headquarters of the party, based in London. • The Board of the Conservative Party is the governing body of the party.	• Each constituency has a Constituency Labour Party (CLP). Smaller local branches choose the local council candidates. • There is a Welsh Labour Party and a Scottish Labour Party within the UK Labour Party. • The National Executive Committee (NEC) is the governing body of the Labour Party. • The Parliamentary Labour Party (PLP) consists of Labour MPs. • 14 trade unions are affiliated to Labour: these are coordinated by the Trade Union and Labour Party Liaison Organisation. • Many socialist societies and groups are affiliated to the Labour Party.	• Unlike the two main parties, the Liberal Democrats use a federal structure. • Members belong to a local party, a regional party and the national party of either England, Wales or Scotland. • The Federal Board is the governing body of the Liberal Democrats, which brings together the national parties. • There is a parliamentary party of the House of Commons, made up of Liberal Democrat MPs. • Members can also join Specified Associated Organisations (SAOs): groups with a particular identity or focus such as Ethnic Minority Liberal Democrats and the Association of Liberal Democrat Engineers and Scientists. They can submit motions to the party conference.
Membership figures	• 124,000 (March 2018).	• 552,000 (June 2017). • Membership numbers increased dramatically since 2015, as a result of the election of Jeremy Corbyn.	• 99,000 (August 2018). • A significant increase in membership numbers since 44,700 in 2014.

Exam tip

Examiners are looking for you to make synoptic links in your essays. Membership figures link to participation and democracy. The general trend of falling membership figures over the past decades might imply that participation is falling, with negative implications for democracy. However, people may be participating in new ways, such as by joining pressure groups. The recent membership growth of Labour and the Liberal Democrats suggests either that the electorate is becoming more engaged or that these parties have become more effective at attracting new members.

Appointing party leaders

The processes for appointing party leaders are given in Table 8.6. All three parties have two rounds, one for the parliamentary party and one for all members using OMOV.

Table 8.6 Choosing and removing party leaders

Conservatives	Labour	Liberal Democrats
• MPs vote on leadership candidates. Their top two choices are presented to the rest of the party. • All party members vote on the remaining two candidates. It is a one member, one vote (OMOV) system, so every vote counts equally. • Theresa May was not voted for by the party membership because her rival withdrew from the contest, leaving May unopposed.	• The Parliamentary Labour Party (PLP) makes nominations first: candidates need to be nominated by at least 10% of the PLP to proceed to the next round. • From September 2018, candidates must also win the support of 5% of local parties or 5% of trade union affiliate members. • All members and 'registered supporters' then vote on candidates, using OMOV and the Alternative Vote system.	• A candidate must be an MP, with the support of at least 10% of Liberal Democrat MPs and backing from at least 20 local parties, with support from at least 200 members. • All members vote using OMOV and the Alternative Vote system. • In September 2018 leader Vince Cable proposed that non-MPs could become leader, and that non-party members could vote in leadership elections.

Labour's use of 'registered supporters' has been controversial. In 2015 supporters who paid £3 were allowed to vote. Some 84% supported Jeremy Corbyn, giving him a significant advantage. In 2016 the fee changed to £25, to prevent leadership elections from being hijacked by people not fully committed to the party.

The Conservative Party gives more power to MPs than Labour or the Liberal Democrats, as only the top two candidates progress to the second round. The eventual winner is therefore likely to have the backing of a significant number of MPs. In contrast, Labour members elected Jeremy Corbyn in 2015 despite his nomination by only 15.5% of MPs.

Choosing parliamentary candidates

All three parties use a similar procedure:
1 Potential candidates are approved by the central organisation of the party.
2 The local party selects candidates from the central party list.
3 Constituency members vote to select the parliamentary candidate.

The three parties have traditionally struggled to select a broad range of candidates, which affects the composition of the House of Commons. They have tried various methods to change this. Labour introduced **all-women shortlists** in 1993, resulting in 101 female Labour MPs being elected in 1997 (in 1992 there were just 60 female MPs in total, 37 of whom were Labour). In September 2017 the party announced plans to use all-women shortlists for almost 50 of its top target seats. The Conservatives have tried priority lists, public hustings and open primaries.
• Priority lists are centrally prepared lists of priority (A-list) candidates, e.g. women and those from ethnic minorities. Priority candidates are offered to the local party when it draws up its shortlist for parliamentary candidates.
• Public hustings are events where parliamentary candidates answer questions on their policies in front of the public, as well as members.

> **All-women shortlists** Lists of solely female candidates for a parliamentary constituency.

> **Revision activity**
>
> Explain the advantages and disadvantages of each of the following:
> • all-women shortlists
> • public hustings
> • open primaries
> • priority lists

● Open primaries are elections in which any registered voter can choose to vote, not just party members.

Establishing party policy

REVISED

The methods for establishing party policy are given in Table 8.7.

Table 8.7 Establishing party policy

Conservatives	Labour	Liberal Democrats
● Top-down process: the leader's team effectively decides what goes in the manifesto. ● Delegates at the party conference do not vote on policy.	● The National Policy Forum (representatives from across the party) agrees on the direction of policy and arranges policy commissions. ● Policies are then voted on at the party conference. ● The leader can use personal authority to win support for his or her policies at conference.	● The Federal Policy Committee (a mix of parliamentarians and other party members) develops policies to be put to the party conference (held twice a year). ● Any member can also make a policy proposal to the party conference. ● The conference votes on all policies and all members can vote.

Exam tip

Questions on party structures and functions are likely to focus on internal democracy (the degree to which ordinary members are involved in decision making within an organisation), so make sure you learn the different ways that members can participate in decision making in each party.

Revision activity

(a) Give each party a score out of five for how much power it gives:
  ● the grassroots
  ● the leader
(b) Which party has the most internal democracy?

Now test yourself

TESTED

5 Which party uses a federal structure?
6 Which party has regularly used all-women shortlists to select parliamentary candidates?
7 Which party does not allow its members to vote on policy at the party conference?

Answers on p. 111

Party funding

Sources and types

REVISED

Party funding is the income received by political parties. It comes from a variety of sources, including membership fees, donations and state funding, as shown in Table 8.8.

Table 8.8 Sources of party funding

Source	Description
Membership fees	Income from these has reduced as membership numbers have fallen since the 1980s.
Small donations from individual members	The fall in membership numbers has also resulted in fewer small donations.

Source	Description
Large donations from wealthy donors	These are a significant source of income, particularly for the Conservative Party. Tony Blair's Labour government was criticised for accepting a £1 million donation from Formula 1 tycoon Bernie Ecclestone in 1997 and then giving Formula 1 an exemption from the ban on tobacco advertising at sporting events.
Trade unions to the Labour Party	Donations from unions are worth millions to Labour, but their value is likely to be reduced by political funding changes in the Trade Union Act 2016.
State funding	Designed to counter the financial advantage enjoyed by the party of government or parties with large funds.

Different types of state funding are described in Table 8.9.

Table 8.9 **Types of state funding**

Type	Description
Short money	State funds paid to opposition parties in the House of Commons to pay for administrative costs and to enable effective scrutiny of the government.
Cranborne money	State funds paid to opposition parties in the House of Lords to pay for administrative costs and to enable effective scrutiny of the government.
Policy Development Grants (PDGs)	Any party with two or more sitting MPs is allocated a share of a £2 million annual fund to help to develop policies.
Funding for election campaigns	State subsidies are given to parties during election campaigns to help with costs.

Typical mistake

Remember that small parties don't receive the same amount of state funding as larger parties. Instead, they are allocated funds according to how many seats they have in parliament and how many votes they won in the last election.

Revision activity

List the advantages and disadvantages of each type of party funding. Remember to consider possible impacts on the party and on UK democracy in general.

Reforms

REVISED

Party funding has seen several recent reforms, as shown in Table 8.10.

Table 8.10 **Reforms to party funding**

Reform	Description
Political Parties, Elections and Referendums Act (PPERA) 2000	• Spending limit on party spending in general election campaigns (£30,000 per constituency). • Donations over £5,000 must be declared to the Electoral Commission.
Political Parties and Elections Act (PPEA) 2009	• Allowed the Electoral Commission to investigate cases and impose fines. • Increased the requirements for establishing the source of political donations.

The media

Relations with the media

REVISED

Party leaders have developed good relationships with media bosses. Tony Blair convinced Rupert Murdoch to switch the *Sun* newspaper's support to Labour; David Cameron met with Murdoch and his associates 26 times during his first 15 months as prime minister.

Newspapers may affect how party leaders are perceived. Ed Miliband was dubbed 'Red Ed' by many newspapers, making it more difficult for him to appeal to centrist voters.

The *Daily Mail* and the *Telegraph* are consistent Conservative supporters, whereas the *Mirror* always favours Labour and the *Guardian* generally does. Other newspapers change their endorsement with each election.

The BBC is a public service broadcaster, so must remain politically neutral. However, it is regularly criticised by both main parties for biased reporting.

An extreme example of this was the aggressive online campaign against Laura Kuenssberg, the BBC's political editor, which resulted in her attending Labour's 2017 conference with bodyguard protection. Critics of Kuenssberg claimed she was prejudiced against Labour.

Social media are increasingly important. Despite the negative portrayal of Jeremy Corbyn by traditional media during the 2017 election, Labour's online campaign allowed it to increase its vote share.

> **Typical mistake**
>
> Don't assume that the media necessarily influence voters. Newspapers certainly try to shape public opinion, but it is unclear how far they influence their readers or whether they simply reflect their readers' views.

Factors affecting electoral outcomes

What factors affect electoral outcomes?

REVISED

Table 8.11 gives some of the issues that affect electoral outcomes.

Table 8.11 Factors affecting electoral outcomes

Factor	Description
Party leader	• Media coverage is very focused on the characteristics of the party leader. • Leaders whose personalities make it difficult to connect with voters (e.g. Gordon Brown and Theresa May) or to impress voters (e.g. Ed Miliband) are likely to have disappointing electoral results.
Funding	• A clear advantage to the Conservatives (wealthy donors). • Traditionally Labour had the benefit of trade union funding, but this has become less significant. • Parties with a chance of being in government have a big advantage as donors think they are worth giving to.
Policies	• Appealing and well-thought-out policies (e.g. New Labour in 1997) have much greater electoral appeal than poorly crafted policies (e.g. the 'dementia tax' in May's 2017 manifesto).
Record	• Governments are judged on their record, e.g. in 1997 John Major's Conservative government was punished for sleaze; in 2015 the Liberal Democrats were punished for their role in the coalition.
The media	• Support from key newspapers such as the *Sun* may be helpful. • Social media are increasingly important, e.g. Corbyn's online campaign in the 2017 election.
Election campaigns	• A well-crafted election campaign can help to secure a landslide (e.g. New Labour in 1997). • A poorly crafted campaign can cause the popularity of a party and its leader to nosedive (e.g. Theresa May in 2017).
Overton window	• The 'window' of public opinion in terms of ideas: any ideas outside the window will not be tolerated by the public. • Parties who keep their policies within the Overton window are much more likely to be elected.
Electoral system	• FPTP favours parties with concentrated geographical support, e.g. the SNP.

Exam practice answers and quick quizzes at **www.hoddereducation.co.uk/myrevisionnotesdownloads**

Now test yourself

8 What is the name for the public funds given to opposition parties in the House of Commons?
9 Who owns the *Sun* newspaper and why is he politically important?
10 What evidence suggests that traditional media are becoming less important in determining electoral outcomes?

Answers on p. 111

Minor parties

Policies of minor parties

Minor parties are those other than the main national parties and include single-issue parties such as UKIP and the Green Party, and nationalist parties such as the SNP and Plaid Cymru. Table 8.12 outlines the main minor parties' policies and their impact on political debates and the political agenda.

Table 8.12 Minor parties

Party	Policies	Impact on political debates and the political agenda
Scottish National Party (SNP)	Independence for Scotland Anti-austerity	• Won a majority in the 2011 Scottish Parliament elections, allowing the SNP to pressure the UK government for a referendum. • Scotland voted to remain in the UK in 2014, so the SNP did not achieve its core objective. • However, SNP membership increased, resulting in a landslide victory in Scotland in the 2015 general election (56 of 59 seats). • The SNP lost seats in 2017 (falling to 35 of 59 seats), but its continuing dominance in Scotland makes it the third largest party in parliament. • First minister Nicola Sturgeon has provided a pro-EU perspective during Brexit negotiations and consistently pointed out that Scotland voted to remain.
UK Independence Party (UKIP)	Supports a 'hard' Brexit Anti-immigration	• Founded in 1993, UKIP gradually built support. • In 2014 it came first in the European Parliament elections, winning 24 seats and pushing the Conservatives into third place. • Fears that many Conservative voters would switch to UKIP in the 2015 general election prompted David Cameron to promise to hold an EU referendum if he won a majority. Cameron won his majority and campaigned for Remain in the 2016 EU referendum. • UKIP's general election results were limited by the FPTP system: it won 3.9 million votes in 2015 but just one seat in the House of Commons. • However, UKIP achieved its core objective when Britain voted to leave the EU in 2016. • Since the 2016 referendum, the party has campaigned for a hard Brexit but struggled to define a clear purpose for itself. It has also lacked a convincing leader since the resignation of Nigel Farage in 2016. • UKIP won fewer than 600,000 votes in the 2017 election and lost its only MP. Its influence has been limited since the referendum.
Plaid Cymru	Independence for Wales Increased investment in Wales, best possible Brexit deal	• Provides a clear voice for Wales and consistently argues in favour of increased public spending. • Prominent during leadership debates in 2015 and 2017 elections. • Struggles for the attention of the media because of its size: it won just four seats in the 2017 general election.

→

Party	Policies	Impact on political debates and the political agenda
Democratic Unionist Party (DUP)	Northern Ireland to remain in the UK Pro-Brexit Against gay marriage and abortion	• Largest unionist party in Northern Ireland. • In government in Northern Ireland with Sinn Fein, until their power-sharing agreement collapsed in 2017. • Won ten seats in the UK Parliament in 2017. • From June 2017 supported the Conservative minority government in a confidence and supply deal. This gave the DUP considerable influence over the Conservative government.
Green Party	Environmental protections and a green economy Investment in public services	• Provides an environmental perspective on all policy areas. • Limited direct influence over policy because of its size: it only won one seat in the 2017 general election. • Encourages other progressive parties to develop environmental policies to compete for 'green' votes. • Helped the Liberal Democrats to win two marginal seats in 2017. The Green Party did not put up candidates and instead encouraged their supporters to vote for the Liberal Democrat candidates, to keep out the Conservatives.

Exam tip

Don't forget that minor parties can still have a significant impact on the political agenda, even if they have very limited representation in parliament. UKIP provides the best example of this: despite only ever winning one seat in a general election (in 2015), it was able to pressurise the Conservatives into calling a referendum on EU membership, transforming the political agenda.

Party system The number of significant political parties operating in a country. Different types of electoral systems produce different party systems. Party systems include one-party (e.g. China), dominant-party (e.g. South Africa), two-party (e.g. USA) and multi-party (e.g. many European countries using proportional representation).

Party systems

Development towards a multi-party system

REVISED

Table 8.13 summarises the **party systems** in the UK.

Table 8.13 What kind of party system does the UK have?

Party system	Definition	UK evidence in favour
Two-party system	• Two significant political parties compete for power. • A typical product of FPTP electoral systems. • Tends to result in single-party majority governments.	• Either the Conservatives or Labour have been in government since 1922. There have been several periods of coalition, most recently with the Liberal Democrats, but the two major parties have provided every prime minister. • Coalition and minority government have traditionally been rare in UK politics. • Only the Conservatives and Labour have a realistic chance of winning the most seats in a UK general election and forming or leading a government. • FPTP has prevented smaller parties such as UKIP from winning a proportional number of seats to their votes. • The 2017 election was described as a 'return to two-party politics' as, together, Labour and the Conservatives won over 80% of the vote: the first time this had happened since the 1980s.

Party system	Definition	UK evidence in favour
Multi-party system	• Multiple significant political parties compete for power. • A typical product of proportional voting systems. • Tends to result in coalitions or minority governments.	• There has been a move away from single-party government in the UK: there was a coalition from 2010 to 2015, and a minority government from 2017. • Smaller parties have played a significant role in government: Liberal Democrats held key positions in government from 2010 to 2015, and from 2017 the Conservatives were dependent on the DUP. • Smaller parties have had a significant impact on UK politics: the SNP's dominance in Scotland from 2015 onwards made it difficult for either the Conservatives or Labour to win a majority and UKIP's rise resulted in the 2016 EU referendum. • Multiple parties hold power across the UK and devolved nations: as of February 2018 the UK, Scotland, Wales and Northern Ireland were all headed by governments from different political parties.

Now test yourself

TESTED

11 Which party made a confidence and supply deal with the Conservatives in 2017?
12 Which minor party has achieved its main aim?
13 Which type of electoral system tends to produce a multi-party system?
14 When did the UK last have a coalition government?

Answers on p. 111

Exam tip

If you are asked which type of party system the UK has, explain that it depends on how you define 'significant' political parties within a party system. If 'significant' means 'leading the UK government', then the UK has a two-party system. If a broader definition is used, such as 'wielding considerable political power', then the UK could now be considered to be a multi-party system.

Summary

You should now have an understanding of:
• the origins, ideas and development of the Conservative, Labour and Liberal Democrat parties
• the party structures and functions of the Conservative, Labour and Liberal Democrat parties
• how party funding works and the rules that regulate it
• factors affecting electoral outcomes, including the relationship between parties and the media
• the policies of minor parties and their impact on political debates and the political agenda
• party systems and the development towards a multi-party system in the UK and its impact on government and policy

Exam practice

AS

1 Explain, with examples, the concept of a multi-party system. [6]

A-level

2 Explain and analyse three features of party funding. [9]
3 'Minor parties have had little impact on the political agenda.' Analyse and evaluate this statement. [25]
4 'Labour is a socialist party.' Analyse and evaluate this statement. [25]

Answers and quick quiz 8 online

ONLINE

9 Pressure groups

Key points

- A pressure group is an organisation that aims to influence political decision making. For example, the NSPCC (National Society for the Prevention of Cruelty to Children) campaigns to encourage the government and parliament to introduce policies and laws to protect children.
- Pressure groups differ from political parties because they seek only to influence those in power, whereas a political party aims to win political power for itself.
- Pressure groups can be very small, such as a local conservation group with only a handful of members. On the other hand, some pressure groups have huge memberships. The Unite union is the largest trade union in the UK, with 1.4 million members. Many pressure groups are part of broader **social movements**.

> **Social movements** Long-term campaigns for the improvement of an aspect of society. Examples include the labour, women's, environmental and gay rights movements, as well as recent internet-based movements such as Occupy and #MeToo. Social movements are less structured and organised than pressure groups and may include pressure groups within them. For example, the environmental movement includes pressure groups Greenpeace and Friends of the Earth.

Typologies

Insider and outsider groups

Insider groups are those that are consulted by the government and therefore have insider status. Insider groups need to be law-abiding with a good public image to retain the trust of the government. For example, the British Medical Association (BMA) is consulted as a matter of course on health-related matters.

Outsider groups are those that are not consulted by the government and instead try to influence political decision making from the outside. Some outsider groups work towards insider status, whereas others are ideologically opposed to the government and happy to remain outsiders. For example, Stop Huntingdon Animal Cruelty (SHAC) used extreme tactics that were incompatible with insider status.

Case study: an insider group

The British Medical Association (BMA)

Table 9.1 **The BMA**

Main aims	• Acts as the doctors' trade union, to improve pay and conditions. • Lobbies the government for improvements to healthcare and public health, e.g. a minimum unit price for alcohol sales, a sugar tax on drinks.
Membership	• 160,000 doctors and medical students.
Methods	• The BMA briefs MPs on health policy, meets with ministers and responds to consultations. • Organised the first full strike by junior doctors (including emergency care) in April 2016, over changes to the junior doctors' contract.
Successes	• Plays a leading role in every public debate about public health and healthcare. • One of the most respected insider groups: influences the government as it develops policies. • In April 2018 the government introduced a sugar tax on fizzy drinks. • In 2017 the government launched a public consultation on an opt-out system for organ donation, which the BMA campaigns for. • From 2002 the BMA campaigned for a smoking ban and was successful in achieving this in 2007. • Campaigned for seatbelts to be compulsory for all occupants of cars: this was finally achieved in 1991.
Failures	• The BMA cancelled plans for a second junior doctors' strike in September 2016 after junior doctors complained that hospitals had not been given long enough to prepare. • The government did not give in to junior doctors: the new contracts were imposed on them in October 2016. • Although the BMA is an effective *promotional group* (see p. 90), its inability to avoid the new contracts suggests that it is less effective as an *interest group*.

Case study: an outsider group

Greenpeace

Table 9.2 **Greenpeace**

Main aims	• Stopping climate change, defending the oceans, protecting forests, eliminating toxins, working for peace and the removal of nuclear weapons, saving the Arctic.
Membership	• Almost 3 million members worldwide, with 130,000 in the UK.
Methods	• A wide range of methods, supported by 2,000 employees and 28 offices across the world and over £300 million in global revenues. • Direct action, e.g. shutting down a coal-fired power station in 2007, putting air pollution masks on the faces of 15 statues in London (including Nelson's Column) in 2016, climbing to the top of the Shard in London in 2013 in protest at plans by the oil company Shell to drill the Arctic. • Patrols the seas, intercepting and challenging whalers, nuclear testers and illegal fishers. Its fleet of ships dwarfs many small countries' navies. • Investigates environmental destruction and produces detailed reports, to influence governments and the public. Proposes solutions to environmental problems. • Has used insider methods more in recent years. It lobbies the UK government and parliament and argues that this works well in combination with direct action methods.

→

Successes	● Government attitudes towards carbon emissions have changed over recent decades. In 2017 the Conservative government announced plans for a lower carbon economy and there is widespread support for green energy. ● Its campaign against microbeads (tiny plastic particles used in toiletries such as toothpaste, which can contaminate water systems) succeeded in 2017 when the government announced it would be introducing a ban. ● Its campaigns against companies have led to some policy changes. For example, it campaigned against Shell because of its Arctic drilling, which included convincing Lego to refuse to work with Shell. In 2015 Shell announced that it would no longer drill in the Arctic.
Failures	● The government's environmental policies do not satisfy activists. London, for example, reached its legal air pollution limit just 1 month in to 2018. For real progress to be made, governments need to take more drastic action. ● Failed to prevent Cairn Energy from drilling for gas off the coast of Greenland. Protesters criticised the traditional Inuit diet of whale and seal meat, turning locals against Greenpeace. ● Some of its methods (including hoaxes and disruptive direct action) have been criticised and can alienate the public and government. ● In 2016 more than 100 Nobel laureates signed a letter criticising Greenpeace for its campaigns against genetically modified organisms (GMOs), arguing that it was anti-science.

Limitations of this classification

Some groups are only consulted occasionally and have little real influence over government. These are known as peripheral insiders.

Insider groups can become outsider groups, and vice versa. Some vary depending on which party is in government. For example, trade unions have traditionally been consulted more by Labour governments.

Even if a group is consulted by government regularly, it may have limited influence if they fundamentally disagree. For example, the BMA failed to convince the government to improve the junior doctors' new contracts.

Promotional and interest groups

REVISED

Promotional groups are those that promote a specific cause, such as the housing and homelessness charity Shelter. They are generally inclusive (members need not have a personal connection to their cause in order to join, unlike interest groups) and altruistic (members join to improve the greater good of society, not for their own benefit). They may build mass memberships to demonstrate public support for their cause.

Interest groups are those that exist to defend the interests of a particular group or section of society. All trade unions are interest groups as they protect the interests of their members, such as the National Education Union (NEU), the UK's largest teaching union.

Limitations of this classification

Some pressure groups do not fit neatly into the promotional and interest group classification. For example, the BMA is a promotional group as it campaigns for better public health, but *also* an interest group as it campaigns for better pay and conditions for its members.

Typical mistake

Don't get confused by the two main classifications of pressure groups and assume that, as there are four different types, a pressure group can belong to only one of the four types. In reality, the two classifications exist alongside each other, so pressure groups are simultaneously either an insider or an outsider group *and* either a promotional or an interest group. For example, the mental health charity Mind has insider status and is a promotional group.

Now test yourself

TESTED

1 What is the difference between a pressure group and a political party?
2 What is the opposite of an insider group?
3 What is the opposite of an interest group?
4 Give two examples of policy areas where the BMA has been successful.
5 Give an example of a BMA campaign that was unsuccessful.
6 How has Greenpeace changed its methods in recent years?

Answers on p. 112

Access points Points at which pressure groups can seek to influence decision-makers. These include local government, devolved governments and legislatures, the UK government, parliament and the judiciary, and (until Brexit) the EU.

Methods used

Working within the system

REVISED

Some pressure groups work within the governmental system by targeting different **access points**. Table 9.3 summarises the methods used to campaign within the governmental system.

Table 9.3 **Working within the governmental system**

Method	Description
Influencing government	• Insider groups try to directly influence ministers and civil servants through contributions to consultations or face-to-face meetings.
Influencing parliament	• Pressure groups lobby MPs to try to influence their votes on government bills. • They try to convince MPs to introduce a private members' bill for their cause. • They can be asked to appear before a backbench committee. Committee reports are considered seriously by the government and often reported by the media. • They may lobby the House of Lords to amend or improve government legislation, to initiate their own legislation or to put an issue on the political agenda by debating it.
Influencing political parties	• Unions have been part of the Labour Party since its formation and make an essential financial contribution. • Some pressure groups attend party conferences to try to influence members and key figures.
Using the courts	• Pressure groups may try to overturn government decisions with legal action using judicial review (see p. 39). • Publicity and changing public opinion may be as important as winning the case. • Chris Grayling, coalition justice secretary, claimed in 2014 that pressure groups were using judicial review too often to delay legislation. The Criminal Justice and Courts Act 2015 made it more difficult for charities to use judicial review.

Typical mistake

Don't overstate the influence of trade unions on the Labour Party. Unions are important financial contributors, but not all Labour Party leaders have been heavily influenced by them. Tony Blair offered 'fairness not favours' to unions. His government faced challenges such as the 2002 firefighters' strikes and was widely criticised by the trade union movement in general.

Working outside the system

Other groups work outside the governmental system, usually by targeting public opinion. Table 9.4 summarises the methods used to campaign outside the governmental system.

Table 9.4 Working outside the governmental system

Method	Description
Appealing to the public	<ul><li>Pressure groups attract public support by using the media.</li><li>They appeal to the public directly using social media and online campaigning.</li><li>They organise demonstrations and marches.</li><li>All pressure groups need public support, but it is especially important for outsider groups.</li></ul>
Background campaigns	<ul><li>Long-term educational and propaganda campaigns are designed to produce significant shifts in public opinion (e.g. the environmental 'reduce, reuse and recycle' campaign or the anti-smoking campaign).</li></ul>
Short-term campaigns	<ul><li>These are aimed at warning the public about a specific problem and trying to solve it.</li><li>The most extreme version was the 'fire brigade campaign', a dramatic campaign designed to rally support quickly and force the government to make rapid change.</li></ul>
Direct action	<ul><li>This is any action taken by a pressure group beyond the usual constitutional methods of campaigning. The aim is to produce a policy change by government.</li><li>Direct action includes commonly used tactics (e.g. marches, demonstrations and strikes) and more unusual headline-grabbing stunts (e.g. climbing buildings and running on to an airport runway).</li><li>Some direct action is legal (e.g. trade union strikes), but some is illegal civil disobedience (e.g. environmental protesters blocking access to fracking sites in 2017).</li><li>In its most extreme form, direct action can include violence (e.g. the English Defence League's protests can turn violent) and harassment (e.g. Stop Huntingdon Animal Cruelty (SHAC) harassed and attacked individuals linked to the Huntingdon Life Sciences animal testing centre) or even terrorism.</li><li>Unlike most direct action, which aims to win publicity and public support, violent direct action is intended to forcibly compel the government to change policy.</li></ul>

Now test yourself

7 What legal method can pressure groups sometimes use to challenge the legality of government action?
8 What is the term for a long-term pressure group campaign that intends to educate the public?
9 What is the term for campaigning that may involve demonstrations, stunts or even violence?

Answers on p. 112

Typical mistake

Don't assume that all direct action is the same. The term covers a range of legal and illegal activities from striking to arson, which may be violent or non-violent.

Exam tip

Learn examples of the different methods used by specific pressure groups, so that you can use these in the exam.

The influence of pressure groups

Factors that affect pressure group influence

REVISED

The factors in Table 9.5 determine how much political influence a pressure group has.

Table 9.5 Factors likely to affect the political influence of pressure groups

Factor	Description
Membership	• Large memberships often have more influence with the government. • Pressure groups with highly regarded memberships are likely to have more influence on politicians, the public and the media (e.g. the BMA is made up of doctors whose professional expertise is widely respected). • However, the government may ignore pressure groups with large memberships (e.g. striking unions) or influential memberships (e.g. the BMA doctors' strike in 2016).
Resources	• Money funds offices, equipment, staff and advertising, helping pressure groups to influence decision-makers. For example, the Confederation of British Industry (CBI) has 13 offices across the UK (and in five areas of the world), helping it to lobby government in the interests of British business. • Resources are needed to fund legal challenges to government policy. Large sums of money are needed for judicial reviews, unless the membership possesses the necessary expertise. For example, Client Earth are activist environmental lawyers who won their third legal victory against the government's air pollution policy in 2018.
Aims	• Limited and easily achievable aims are more likely to be met. For example, the Snowdrop Campaign was set up after the Dunblane massacre of 1996 and aimed to ban private ownership of handguns in the UK. This was straightforward to achieve and an Act of Parliament was passed in 1997.
Public support	• Public support helps to convince politicians to support and prioritise the pressure group's cause. For example, the Snowdrop Campaign had huge public support, so MPs and government were keen to ban handgun ownership.
Methods	• Pressure groups that target the appropriate access points (see p. 91) for their cause will have a better chance of influencing political decision-makers. • Direct action needs to be handled carefully: stunts can bring media attention and help to influence politicians, but violent and dangerous campaigning is likely to alienate decision-makers and the public. • A good example of counterproductive methods is the SHAC group, which was forced to end its campaign in 2014 and 'reassess' its methods. These had been directed at people linked to animal testing and included blackmail, damage to property, sending hoax bombs and items supposedly contaminated with AIDS and falsely exposing staff as paedophiles. The result was heavy prison sentences for some of its members and new laws to protect animal testing services.
Celebrity endorsement	• Endorsement can bring publicity to an issue that might otherwise be overlooked by politicians. For example, Joanna Lumley's commitment to the Gurkha Justice Campaign ensured national media coverage of this cause. She met prime minister Gordon Brown, whose government announced in 2009 that Gurkha veterans who met certain requirements would be allowed to live in the UK.

→

Factor	Description
Links with political parties	• Trade union donations are hugely important to Labour, and provided much of the funding for its 2017 election campaign. However, trade union membership figures have fallen, and union influence may be curtailed further by the Trade Union Act 2016. • Political parties can approach pressure groups to gain support for a new policy. • Endorsement from a respected pressure group can boost the policy's credibility. For example, the BMA supported Labour's 2007 smoking ban.
Links with government	• Pressure groups are generally experts in their area, whereas civil servants or ministers may not be. This expertise can be helpful to the government. • Insider status can allow pressure groups to directly influence government policy, as was the case with the BMA and the 2007 smoking ban. • Different governments will be influenced by different pressure groups. For example, Labour governments are traditionally more influenced by trade unions than Conservative governments.
Relationship with the media	• Most pressure groups aim to attract publicity from the media, particularly when carrying out direct action. They inform the media of what they are planning so that journalists can be there to document it. • Media support can put pressure on politicians. For example, the media supported the Snowdrop Campaign. • Media criticism of pressure groups helps the government to justify ignoring their demands. For example, most newspapers criticised the BMA's 2016 doctors' strike.

Typical mistake

Media *attention* is not the same as media *support*. Both the Animal Liberation Front and the English Defence League have received considerable media attention but are widely condemned by the media for their extreme tactics.

Typical mistake

Publicity does not automatically guarantee influence. The biggest UK public protest, the 2003 march of over 1 million people against the Iraq War, did not change government policy.

Exam tip

You may be asked how pressure groups influence the political agenda. This is slightly different to being asked how they influence the government, as the political agenda simply means the most important political issues of the day and can be determined by the public or the media, rather than by the government. An issue can be high on the political agenda but still be ignored by the government, such as the opposition to the Iraq War in 2003.

Exam tip

In an essay about pressure group success, you need to evaluate what makes pressure groups successful. This means considering the different factors in Table 9.5, deciding which is the most important and justifying your decision.

If you find it difficult to decide which factor is the most important in determining pressure group influence, look for links between the different factors. If one factor has more links than any others, it may well be the most important. Explaining these connections will also give you marks for synoptic links.

Exam tip

If you are writing an essay about pressure group success, make sure you use examples effectively. Students often make statements about pressure groups (e.g. 'the BMA is an insider group, which makes it successful') without giving examples of *how* the pressure group has been successful (e.g. 'In 2007 the Labour government imposed a smoking ban. This is an example of how the BMA used its insider status to achieve success, as it lobbied the government for change and was consulted as part of the legislative process').

Revision activity

(a) Write the different factors that contribute to pressure group influence around the sides of a piece of paper, leaving space between them.
(b) Summarise the information in Table 9.5 into no more than 25 words for each factor and add these to your diagram.
(c) Make links between the different factors, adding these to your diagram and writing an explanation for each one.

Other influences on government and parliament

Other influences

There are other influences on government and parliament, as shown in Table 9.6.

Table 9.6 Other influences on government and parliament

Influence	Description
Think-tanks	• Think-tanks are organisations that exist purely to develop new policies. • They are funded privately by donations from individuals, groups or business. • Some have a clear position on the political spectrum (e.g. the Fabian Society is left of centre and aims to 'shape the future of the left'; the Adam Smith Institute is right of centre and supports neo-liberal free-market ideas). • Others seek to be independent and neutral (e.g. Chatham House, an international policy think-tank). • Think-tanks do not campaign for political parties but instead aim to convince political parties or the government to adopt their ideas. • Political policies were traditionally developed within political parties, but Tony Blair increased the use of think-tanks. • Many politicians have close links with think-tanks (e.g. Iain Duncan Smith, former leader of the Conservatives, set up the Centre for Social Justice in 2004). • Think-tanks produce detailed policy and research, which can be used by political parties. • They may be consulted by political parties when formulating policy. • They frequently appear in the media to comment on policy debates.
Lobbyists	• Lobbyists are political operatives who are paid to influence the government. • They are usually employed by corporations or wealthy pressure groups. • They arrange meetings with influential politicians and try to convince them to support the aims of their employer. • Lobbying has grown in the UK over the last two decades. There are more than 100 lobbying firms in the UK, but it remains a much bigger industry in the USA. • Many former UK politicians or political advisers become lobbyists, using their contacts to get access to current government officials. • In the 2015 'cash for access' scandal, Jack Straw (Labour) and Sir Malcolm Rifkind (Conservative), both former foreign secretaries, were revealed to be prepared to lobby for companies in return for large sums of money. Although legal, this demonstrated the access that lobbyists can have.
Corporations	• Corporations may be invited by the government to contribute to policy discussions and to help produce legislation relevant to their business. • They lobby the government (often using professional lobbyists) for favourable conditions of business such as low taxes, fewer regulations and better infrastructure. • They may threaten to leave the UK entirely or relocate some of their business to another country if the government does not meet their demands. • Large multinational companies (e.g. Google and Amazon) can structure their business across several countries, resisting UK government attempts to make them pay more tax. • Governments are wary of alienating big businesses, as they are crucial to the economy and employ many people. They also generate tax revenue. • Many owners of large corporations also make donations to political parties, particularly the Conservatives. • Most big companies actively campaigned for Remain during the 2016 EU referendum (although a minority supported Leave). However, they were ignored by the British public. • Many corporations fund think-tanks that support their aims (e.g. the Institute of Economic Affairs (IEA) opposed plain cigarette packaging and received funding from British American Tobacco).

→

Influence	Description
The media	• Governments are scrutinised by the media, and are keen to attract positive reports: communication with the media is a key priority for every government. • Government ministers often have personal links with key figures in the media (e.g. in 2012 the close friendship between prime minister David Cameron and Rebekah Brooks, former editor of the *News of the World* and the *Sun*, was revealed). • Support from newspapers can help governments win elections and increase enthusiasm for their policies within parliament and the country.

Now test yourself

TESTED

10 Which of the main political parties is most likely to favour trade unions?
11 How has Client Earth successfully challenged the government?
12 What is a lobbyist?

Answers on p. 112

Pluralism

What is pluralism?

REVISED

Pluralism describes a situation in which different groups, including pressure groups, compete equally for power and influence. Power is therefore spread across different groups in society. It is the opposite of elitism – the idea that powerful elites dominate society and government.

Table 9.7 assesses whether pressure groups are good for democracy.

Table 9.7 Are pressure groups good for democracy?

Yes	No
• The pluralist interpretation is that pressure groups are an essential part of democracy as they allow different sections of society to have their views heard by government. • Pressure groups allow people to focus on one issue that concerns them (e.g. the environment), although that might not be their prime concern in an election. It is important that the government is held to account for the things that do not win elections but which still matter. • Pressure groups allow people to participate in democracy at any time, rather than just during an election campaign every 5 years. • Many pressure groups have more members than political parties, suggesting they are more relevant to the public. • Pressure groups provide the government with information and statistics it might otherwise not discover. This is good for democracy as it makes the government better informed. • To prevent unions from striking with low internal support, the Trade Union Act 2016 introduced a minimum turnout of 50% for strike ballots and a 40% threshold of support for emergency services. Strikes should now have a stronger democratic mandate from within the pressure group.	• The elitist interpretation is that pressure groups are undemocratic: they give a louder voice to the most powerful. Rich, educated and well-connected people are better able to form influential pressure groups than the poor and disadvantaged and can afford to hire expensive lobbyists and lawyers. • Pressure groups often have limited internal democracy so do not truly represent their members. Decisions can be made by the leadership without consulting members. • Unlike political parties, pressure groups are unaccountable to the electorate. • Pressure groups focus on one particular issue to the exclusion of everything else. They may prevent politicians from delivering joined-up government (see p. 29). • Violent and aggressive campaigning methods (used by a small minority of pressure groups) are contrary to the rule of law and liberal democracy. • The New Right interpretation (associated with Thatcher's Conservative government) argued that trade union strikes and direct action were an attempt to undermine the democratic state. Douglas Hurd (Thatcher's foreign secretary) described pressure groups as 'serpents that strangle efficient government'.

Exam practice answers and quick quizzes at **www.hoddereducation.co.uk/myrevisionnotesdownloads**

Now test yourself

13 Why do pluralists think that pressure groups are good for democracy?

14 Which of the main political parties has been most critical of trade unions?

15 Why could it be argued that pressure groups are more important for participation than political parties?

Answers on p. 112

Summary

You should now have an understanding of:

- different typologies of pressure groups, including insider and outsider groups, promotional groups and interest groups
- insider and outsider group case studies: the successes and failures of the BMA and Greenpeace
- pressure group methods, including those used within the governmental system and those used outside the governmental system
- how pressure groups influence the government
- other influences on the government and parliament, including think-tanks, lobbyists, corporations and the media
- the importance of pressure groups as part of a pluralist society
- arguments concerning the impact of pressure groups on democracy

Exam practice

AS

1 Explain, with examples, the concept of a promotional group. [6]

A-level

2 Explain and analyse three features of outsider groups. [9]

3 Explain and analyse three ways that pressure groups can influence government. [9]

4 'Pressure groups play a crucial role in the UK's democratic system.' Analyse and evaluate this statement. [25]

Answers and quick quiz 9 online

10 The European Union

Key points

- The European Union (EU) consists of 28 member states (27 after Britain leaves the EU).
- Different EU institutions are responsible for executive (government), legislative (making laws) and judicial (interpreting and applying the law) actions.
- The EU's aims include peace, removing internal borders and achieving freedom and economic growth while promoting different cultures and languages.
- In June 2016 Britain voted to leave the EU.
- The EU has played a significant role in UK politics, both before and since the EU referendum.

> **Supranational body** An organisation that exists separately from national governments. In the case of the EU, national governments agree to give power to its supranational bodies and to accept their decisions.
>
> **Intergovernmental body** An organisation made up of members of different national governments.

Institutions

Key institutions

Table 10.1 summarises the institutions that comprise the EU.

Table 10.1 EU institutions

Institution	Role	Significance
European Commission	Initiates EU legislation Drafts the EU budget and allocates funding Represents EU in international negotiations	**Supranational body** 28 commissioners, one from each EU country (after Brexit this will fall to 27) Commissioners are not directly elected: national governments nominate commissioners and the European Council nominates the president of the Commission. Nominees are confirmed by the European Parliament
Council of the European Union	Main decision-making body of EU (together with the European Parliament) Coordinates policies of EU nations Approves legislation from the Commission (as does the European Parliament) Approves the EU budget (as does the European Parliament)	**Intergovernmental body** Government ministers from each of the member nations attend and make decisions together Ten different types of meetings, attended by the appropriate ministers, e.g. finance ministers at the meeting on economic and financial affairs
European Council	Decides the direction of the EU and policy priorities	Intergovernmental body Heads of government (or state) for all EU nations meet four times a year

Institution	Role	Significance
European Parliament	Approves legislation from the Commission (as does the Council of the European Union) Approves the EU budget (as does the Council of the European Union) Provides democratic supervision of EU institutions	The EU's only directly elected body 751 Members of the European Parliament (MEPs) Each EU nation is allocated a number of seats in the European Parliament that reflects its size, e.g. Germany has 96 and Cyprus has 6
Court of Justice of the European Union (CJEU)	Judiciary of the EU Interprets the law and ensures it is applied in the same way across the EU Rules against EU nations that infringe the law Ensures that the EU acts appropriately and in accordance with its own laws	Judges appointed by national governments

The EU system of government (see Figure 10.1) features shared executive powers (the European Commission is the main executive branch but the Council of the European Union also has some executive powers) and shared legislative powers (exercised by both the European Parliament and the Council of the European Union). The Council of the European Union is made up of government ministers from member nations and therefore effectively acts under the authority of the European Council (the less frequent formal meetings of heads of government of EU nations). This means that both the democratically elected European Parliament and the democratically elected national governments have a direct role in the legislative process (see Figure 10.2). The European Council is responsible for making big strategic decisions (such as a change to a treaty or a major shift in policy direction), but it only meets a few times a year. More routine decision making is carried out by the Commission and the Council of the European Union, along with the European Parliament when changes to legislation are required. The Court of Justice stands alone as the EU's independent judiciary.

> **Typical mistake**
>
> Don't confuse the Court of Justice of the European Union with the European Court of Human Rights (ECtHR). The Court of Justice is an EU institution, whereas the ECtHR is not.

> **Typical mistake**
>
> The Council of the European Union and the European Council are easily muddled up. The Council of the European Union is composed of government ministers and approves legislation and makes decisions on specific areas of policy. The European Council is composed of government leaders and is responsible for overall EU strategy, which is often determined by negotiations and bargaining between the most important EU members.

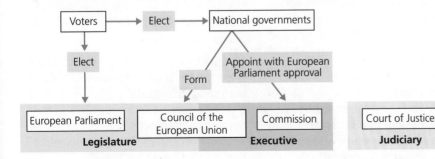

Figure 10.1 **The EU system of government**

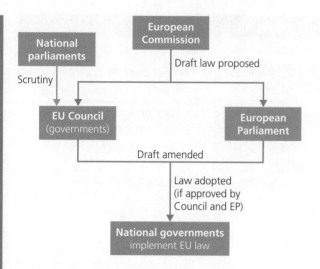

Figure 10.2 **The EU legislative process**

Now test yourself

TESTED

1 Which EU institution has the power to initiate legislation?
2 Which is the only directly elected EU institution?
3 Which EU body is responsible for the overall strategic direction of the EU and is made up of the leaders of member states?
4 What is the name of the EU's judiciary?

Answers on p. 112

Aims and achievements

What are the EU's main aims and achievements?

REVISED

The main aims and achievements of the EU are given in Table 10.2.

Table 10.2 **Aims and achievements of the EU**

Aims (taken and adapted from the EU's website)	Evidence that the aim has been achieved	Evidence that the aim has not been achieved
Promote peace, the values of the EU and the wellbeing of its citizens	• The member nations of the EU have not fought each other since the end of the Second World War. • Rising living standards and economic growth have coincided with the EU's existence. • Democracy and the rule of law operate in EU countries.	• The EU faces new threats from an increasingly aggressive Russia, an unstable middle east and home-grown terrorism. • The rise of populist anti-EU parties over the last decade shows the frustration felt by citizens who feel the EU has not enriched their lives. • The EU has been criticised for having a **democratic deficit**.
Freedom, security and justice without internal borders	• All EU countries are part of the single market, in which the **four freedoms** apply. • 22 of the 28 EU member states are members of the Schengen Area, in which there are no border controls between countries.	• Not all EU countries are in the Schengen Area: the UK and the Republic of Ireland both chose to opt out. • Border checks can be reimposed by Schengen members in the event of a security threat, as France did after the 2015 Paris terror attacks.

Aims (taken and adapted from the EU's website)	Evidence that the aim has been achieved	Evidence that the aim has not been achieved
	● EU countries work together on policing and anti-terrorism, including using the European Arrest Warrant to arrest criminals across the EU.	● Since the 2015 migration crisis, border controls have been reintroduced by Schengen states including Austria and Denmark, to stop migrants from the middle east and Africa arriving via other countries in the Schengen Area.
Balanced economic growth, a competitive market economy with full employment and environmental protection	● The EU has led the development of competitive economies, encouraging eastern European countries to transition from communist states to flourishing capitalist economies. ● EU environmental regulations are generally stricter than those of individual nations (e.g. the UK), resulting in higher standards of air quality, beach cleanliness and protection of species and habitats.	● The 2008 economic crisis damaged the economies of EU nations. ● Unemployment rose dramatically in some EU countries (20.9% in Greece in January 2018) and the overall unemployment rate is higher in the EU than in the USA (7.3% in the EU in December 2017, compared to 4.1% in the USA).
Combat social exclusion and discrimination	● EU law protects individuals' human rights. ● EU citizens have freedom of movement and cannot be discriminated against.	● The migration crisis exposed some of the prejudice within EU countries, demonstrated by attacks on refugee housing. ● In May 2018 the right-wing government in Hungary announced legislation to restrict help for asylum seekers.
Scientific and technological progress	● The European Research Area encourages sharing of scientific knowledge, research and skills. ● Billions of euros of EU funding are spent on science and technology. ● The European Research Council's investments in scientific research have led to numerous breakthroughs.	● EU countries invest less in research and development than their main competitors (e.g. the USA and China). ● The USA is more effective at turning research and new technology into world-leading businesses, e.g. Facebook and Google.
Economic, social and territorial cohesion and solidarity among member countries	● By **pooling sovereignty**, EU nations have been able to act as a united front. ● The EU is the second largest economy in the world. By working together, EU nations make better trade deals with non-EU countries than if they negotiated alone. ● The single market is the largest in the world. It created more than 2.5 million jobs from 1992 to 2006 and has encouraged economic growth. ● The EU protects workers' rights. ● The EU provides hundreds of billions of euros of funding to less economically developed regions (e.g. Wales) to try to reduce disparities across the EU.	● Brexit shows the limitations of EU solidarity, as the UK voted to leave. ● Strong anti-EU voices in other countries (e.g. Marine Le Pen in France) have called for their own referendum on EU membership. ● The EU's goal of 'ever-closer union' has been enthusiastically promoted by France and Germany but criticised by leaders of some other EU countries such as Italy and the Netherlands. ● The single market has been criticised for over-regulating smaller businesses. ● After the EU enlarged in 2004 to include ten new states, high levels of migration from eastern European countries to the UK led to calls for an end to freedom of movement.

→

Aims (taken and adapted from the EU's website)	Evidence that the aim has been achieved	Evidence that the aim has not been achieved
		• Despite being given more than £245 million from the EU than it pays in each year, Wales voted to leave the EU. • Socioeconomic inequality is growing in the EU.
Respect its rich cultural and linguistic diversity	• The EU has 24 official languages and provides funding for language learning. • Every year two EU cities are selected as European capitals of culture.	• The EU has been criticised for its large expenditure on translation services. • The EU's goal that every citizen should speak two languages in addition to their mother tongue had been achieved by only 25% of people in 2014. • A number of EU countries (e.g. France in 2010 and Denmark in 2018) have introduced a ban on face-coverings worn by some Muslim women.
Establish an economic and monetary union whose currency is the euro	• 19 member states (collectively known as the Eurozone) use the euro. • The euro is the world's second most-traded currency (after the dollar).	• The EU's second biggest economy, the UK, chose not to join the euro. • The 2008 economic crisis exposed the problems caused by a range of very different economies sharing the same currency. • This led to a long period of recession or near-recession for the Eurozone and forced austerity (cuts) in countries such as Greece which fuelled the rise of populist anti-EU parties.

Democratic deficit The idea that the EU is not sufficiently democratic because most of its institutions are not directly elected.

Four freedoms Within the EU single market, these are the free movement of goods, services, people and capital.

Pooling sovereignty The idea of strengthening a country's resources by combining them with those of partner countries, giving the EU authority to make decisions on their behalf.

Typical mistake

The Schengen Area and the single market are not the same thing. All EU member states are part of the single market, in which the four freedoms operate. Most EU nations have also chosen to join the Schengen Area, a group of 26 European countries (22 of whom are EU members) in which there are no internal borders.

Typical mistake

Don't assume that the democratic deficit debate means that the EU is anti-democratic. The EU is based on democratic values: the European Parliament is elected and any country wishing to join the EU must be a democracy. The democratic deficit results from the way that many of the members of its institutions are selected by national governments. Institutions such as the European Commission and the Council of the European Union are not directly accountable to the electorate.

Typical mistake

Although the EU has its own currency, the euro, EU member states do not have to use it if they prefer to retain their own currency.

Revision activity

1 Give the EU a score out of ten for how effectively it has achieved each of the aims listed in Table 10.2.
2 Make a list of reasons to explain the EU's success or failure in achieving the aims given in Table 10.2.

Now test yourself

TESTED

5 Which of the four freedoms allows high levels of immigration to the UK from EU countries?
6 When was the last time that EU member states fought each other in a major war?
7 Which event caused unemployment to rise in many EU countries?
8 Which event has caused some EU nations in the Schengen Area to reintroduce border controls?

Answers on p. 112

The impact of the EU on UK politics

Cautious involvement: 1970s–1990s

REVISED

- The UK joined the European Economic Community (EEC), the precursor to the EU, in 1973, some 15 years after it was formed.
- In addition to joining late, UK politicians remained divided over membership. The Labour government held a referendum in 1975, with the result that the UK stayed in.
- Labour later moved to the left and in 1981 the party committed to leave the EEC if it won the general election (it did not). This prompted four high-profile members to leave Labour and form a new pro-EU party, the Social Democratic Party (SDP), which merged with the Liberal Party to become the Liberal Democrats in 1988.
- UK governments negotiated an EU budget rebate in 1981 and a selection of opt-outs from EU policies and treaties. These reduced the impact of EU membership on the UK compared to other EU countries.

Rising euroscepticism: 1990s–2016

REVISED

- Conservative prime minister John Major (1990–97) found his government plagued by rebellions carried out by eurosceptic Conservative MPs.
- The dominant political figure of this period, prime minister Tony Blair (1997–2007), was a europhile, but the British political elite lacked the degree of consensus over membership found in most other EU countries. Eurosceptics existed in both the Labour and the Conservative parties.
- Tony Blair authorised the 2004 EU expansion, but the resulting high level of immigration from eastern Europe was criticised by right-wing newspapers such as the *Daily Mail* and the *Sun*.
- The UK Independence Party (UKIP) was first founded in the 1990s, but grew significantly under the leadership of the populist Nigel Farage (2006–09, 2010–16), who criticised mass immigration, the democratic deficit and the bureaucracy of the EU.
- In 2014 UKIP won the UK elections to the European Parliament, pushing the Conservatives into third place.

A divided Britain: the 2016 EU referendum

REVISED

In an attempt to prevent UKIP from taking votes from the Conservatives, prime minister David Cameron included an EU referendum in the

Conservatives' 2015 general election manifesto. This meant that when the Conservatives won the general election, Cameron was committed to hold a referendum.

The Conservatives were very divided over EU membership, with Cameron and many prominent Conservatives campaigning for Remain, whereas high-profile Conservatives such as Boris Johnson and Michael Gove played a leading role in the Leave campaign. There were also divisions within Labour, although most MPs supported Remain. The Liberal Democrats and the Scottish National Party (SNP) both supported Remain.

Most 'expert' opinion (e.g. economists and business leaders) argued that leaving the EU would damage the UK. The Leave campaign was criticised for misleading claims about the impact of Brexit on the UK's finances. The Remain campaign focused on the economic risks of Brexit, rather than addressing voters' broader concerns by identifying the positive benefits of EU membership.

The final result (52% Leave, 48% Remain) was a terrible shock to many Remainers and highlighted divisions across the UK in terms of age, social class, education and geography (see Figures 10.3 and 10.4). Older, working-class, less-educated, English and Welsh voters were each more likely to vote Leave than those who were younger, middle-class, university-educated and living in London, Scotland or Northern Ireland.

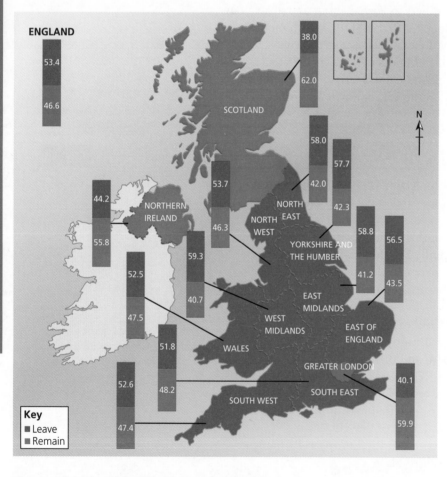

Figure 10.3 **The 2016 EU referendum results**

Source: Electoral Commission

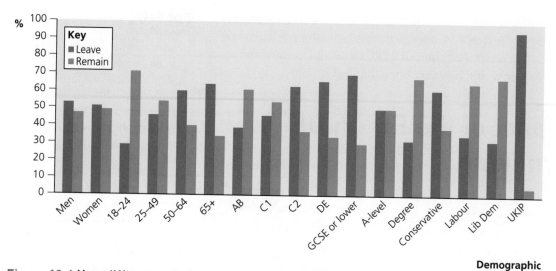

Demographic

Figure 10.4 How different categories of people voted in the 2016 EU referendum

Source: YouGov (**www.tinyurl.com/zvsb5bb**)

Post-referendum politics

The first impact of the Brexit vote was David Cameron's resignation as prime minister. After his leading role in the Remain campaign, he felt he could not carry on as leader after the result was declared. He was replaced by Theresa May, who was also a Remainer but had played a less prominent role in the referendum campaign. May has balanced Brexiteers and Remainers in her cabinet in an attempt to maintain support from both sides of the party. The appointment in 2016 of Boris Johnson as foreign secretary and May's reluctance to remove him from his position after several high-profile gaffes demonstrated the extent to which the prime minister's selection of cabinet ministers was constrained by Brexit. In July 2018, both Johnson and Brexit secretary David Davis resigned from the cabinet as they felt unable to accept collective responsibility for the government's proposed Brexit deal.

The Brexit negotiations became the top item on the political agenda following the referendum. They overshadow all other political initiatives within parliament and dominate government activity.

The referendum result was a challenge to parliamentary sovereignty, as the majority of MPs were Remainers but the nation voted to Leave.

The government had hoped to avoid asking parliament to vote on Article 50, but was frustrated by a January 2017 ruling by the Supreme Court. By requiring parliament to make the final decision, the Supreme Court made it clear that parliament is still sovereign, regardless of the referendum result. However, the majority of MPs ignored their own views and voted to trigger Article 50. This shows the importance of **popular sovereignty** in modern British politics.

Brexit could be extremely damaging for the union of UK nations and threatens the future of devolution. The SNP have called for a second Scottish independence referendum once the Brexit deal has been made. Northern Ireland faces the prospect of having border controls imposed between itself and the Republic of Ireland, which would horrify Republicans and potentially put the hard-won peace process at risk.

> **Popular sovereignty**
> Applies to a situation in which the people are the supreme authority and the government receives its authority from them. In theory, all representative democracies are based on popular sovereignty, as the people elect their representatives to act on their behalf. There is therefore only a tension between popular and parliamentary sovereignty when the people's wishes are different to those of their elected representatives, as in the case of Brexit.

The difficulty of negotiating a good deal for the UK is considerable and explains why May did not face a leadership challenge after her mistaken decision to call a snap general election in 2017. Leading Conservatives knew the job of leader would be easier once the deal is done.

The impact of the EU on UK policy making

Impacts on policy making

REVISED

Table 10.3 outlines some of the policy areas that have been affected by the EU.

Table 10.3 Impacts on policy making

Policy area	Impacts of the EU on UK policy making
Economy	<ul><li>The UK considered joining the euro under New Labour, but decided not to in 2003. This allowed the UK to retain its own economic policy, giving it some protection from the problems faced by the Eurozone after the 2008 economic crisis.</li><li>The UK receives about £1 billion of EU funding for less developed regions (e.g. Wales), which has allowed investment in a range of structural projects designed to support economic development and employment.</li><li>The UK is a net contributor to the EU budget, so UK governments had to pay more into the EU than they received back.</li><li>The EU negotiated trade policies on behalf of the UK and other members, so after Brexit the UK will have more freedom to make its own trade deals. However, it will have less influence as it has a much smaller economy than the EU.</li></ul>
Agriculture	<ul><li>The Common Agricultural Policy (CAP) provides EU subsidies (funding support) for all EU farmers.</li><li>The CAP has prevented the UK from developing its own farming policies, which might suit its needs better. Under the CAP, many wealthy UK landowners receive funding and the system has also been criticised for promoting farming that damages the environment.</li></ul>
Fisheries	<ul><li>The Common Fisheries Policy (CFP) has prevented the UK from protecting its fishing industry from competition. All EU fishers have access to British waters, which has damaged UK fishing.</li></ul>
Environment	<ul><li>EU environmental laws forced UK governments to introduce more environmentally friendly policies, leading to lower levels of air and water pollution and the protection of species and habitats.</li></ul>
Social policy	<ul><li>EU social policy has led to increased rights for UK workers, e.g. paid holidays.</li><li>EU laws and initiatives to promote gender equality have had a big impact on UK policy, leading to shared parental leave, the outlawing of gender pay discrimination and maternity discrimination, and funding for gender equality and anti-violence against women work.</li></ul>
Policing and security	<ul><li>EU membership has allowed the UK to develop a coordinated policing and security strategy with other members.</li><li>The UK has benefitted from membership of Europol (the EU's law-enforcement agency, which acts as a hub for information sharing between national police forces and security services) and from the use of the European Arrest Warrant.</li><li>The government is keen to continue with these arrangements, or similar, after Brexit.</li></ul>

Exam practice answers and quick quizzes at **www.hoddereducation.co.uk/myrevisionnotesdownloads**

Policy area	Impacts of the EU on UK policy making
Immigration	• Freedom of movement prevented UK governments from restricting immigration from EU countries. In the year before the 2016 referendum, net migration to the UK from EU countries was around 190,000. • Since 2010, the Conservative Party has promised to cut net migration to 'the tens of thousands'. Although this pledge was popular with voters, it was impossible to achieve as long as the UK remained in the EU. • Brexit may give UK governments more freedom to introduce immigration controls, although some experts argue that immigration is essential for the health of the economy.

After Brexit the UK government will need to develop independent policies in regard to each policy area. Many Remainers fear that the environmental and social benefits of EU membership will be removed or eroded after Britain leaves the EU. Brexiteers argue that there is no reason why Britain cannot pursue similar policies alone. The UK government has pledged to maintain many of the same funding commitments (e.g. the CAP) for the initial years following Brexit, but in the longer term it will likely develop its own unique policies that may differ significantly from those of the EU.

Now test yourself

TESTED

9 Which UK political party has been most affected by divisions over Britain's EU membership?
10 What percentage of UK voters chose to leave the EU in the 2016 referendum?
11 How did the 2016 referendum result affect the leadership of the UK government?
12 Which high-profile Brexiteer was first given the job of foreign secretary in Theresa May's cabinet?

Answers on p. 112

Summary

You should now have an understanding of:
• the executive power in the EU, which is shared between the European Commission and the Council of the European Union
• the legislative power in the EU, which is shared by the Council of the European Union and the European Parliament
• the European Council and its responsibility for major strategic decisions
• the European Court of Justice and its role as the EU's judiciary
• the EU's successes in achieving many of its aims, including peace, freedom, diversity and long-term economic growth
• events such as the 2008 economic crisis, the 2015 migration crisis and the 2016 UK EU referendum result, which have demonstrated some of the EU's limitations
• the EU as a divisive issue in UK politics and the extent to which the 2016 referendum result has put Brexit and its impact on the UK at the top of the political agenda

Exam tip

There are lots of opportunities to make synoptic links in a question about the impact of the EU. Consider the effect on issues such as political parties, government, the constitution and democracy.

Revision activity

1 Using Table 10.3, make a list of policies that were developed by political parties and governments as a result of the EU.
2 Make a note of the different ways in which the EU has affected:
• political parties
• government (including the role of the prime minister and cabinet)
• the constitution (including the threat to devolution and the challenge to parliamentary sovereignty)
• democracy (including the democratic deficit and popular sovereignty)

Exam practice

AS

1 Explain, with examples, the role of the European Commission.   [6]

A-level

2 Explain and analyse three ways that the EU has had an impact on UK politics.   [9]

Read the following extract.

The EU has struggled to meet the challenges of the twenty-first century. The 2004 expansion of the EU to include less affluent eastern European countries made freedom of movement a contentious issue, particularly in the UK. The 2008 economic crisis pushed the Eurozone almost to breaking point, leading to austerity measures being centrally imposed on weaker countries such as Greece and high levels of unemployment in the most-affected nations. The 2015 migration crisis led to increased resistance to open borders in the Schengen Area and the rise of populist right-wing parties with anti-migrant messages. The result of the UK's 2016 EU referendum shows the frailty of this organisation, as one of its most powerful countries has chosen to leave. Calls for referendums in France and Italy have intensified since the Brexit vote, leading observers to wonder if the EU will lose another member in the future.

However, such a negative view of the EU may be too pessimistic. It is perhaps unsurprising that the EU has struggled with the economic crisis and the migration crisis, as these are two of the biggest challenges to face Europe for many years. Crucially, the EU survived both of these problems. Furthermore, the defection of the UK could be seen as the end product of a long-term process of British disenchantment with the EU, rather than a result of broader failings. Since its creation, the EU has enjoyed decades of peace and stability combined with economic growth and freedom for its citizens: surely a testament to its long-term success.

Source: Original material, 2018

3 Analyse, evaluate and compare the arguments in the above extract over the extent to which the EU has achieved its aims.   [25]
4 'Despite claims of a democratic deficit, the EU is a profoundly democratic organisation.' Analyse and evaluate this statement.   [25]

Answers and quick quiz 10 online

ONLINE

Now test yourself answers

Chapter 1

1 Because parliament can leave the EU simply by repealing an earlier law and passing a new law: the European Union (Withdrawal) Act
2 Parliamentary privilege
3 1 year (it was previously 2 years)
4 The Cabinet Manual
5 No, but breaking one can often lead to major crisis for parliament/government.
6 It is absolute, universal and fundamental.
7 The prime minister's
8 The Information Commissioner's Office (ICO)
9 37%
10 The European Convention on Human Rights (ECHR)
11 The House of Lords
12 (a) Bill of Rights 1689
   (b) Parliament Act 1911
   (c) Act of Settlement 1701
   (d) Fixed-term Parliaments Act 2011
   (e) Magna Carta 1215
   (f) Freedom of Information Act 2000
13 (a) Individual, as this is about practising one's religious faith as many Christians disapprove of same-sex relationships.
   (b) Collective, as this is all about the rights of a group of workers as a whole.
   (c) Collective, as this is about the rights of a free press to publish stories they feel are in the national interest.
   (d) Individual, as this is about one person asserting their rights not to be discriminated against (although it could also be argued that it reflects the desire to enforce the collective rights of disabled people as a whole).
   (e) Collective, as it is about a group of parents demanding what they see as fair treatment for their children (although it also has aspects of the collective right not to discriminate on the grounds of gender).

Chapter 2

1 650
2 Church of England bishops
3 Law-passing

4 Select committees have general oversight of government departments whereas public bill committees oversee individual parliamentary bills.
5 Respond to it (within 60 days)
6 A leading MP from the opposition
7 It is too adversarial and theatrical, with a rowdy and often boorish atmosphere.
8 It can lead to the downfall of the government.
9 Not that important; although it formally makes a bill into a law, it is purely ceremonial and a formality.
10 The second reading
11 (a) Second reading
   (b) Royal assent
   (c) Committee stage
   (d) Third reading
   (e) Report stage

Chapter 3

1 Weekly
2 The prime minister
3 Five
4 2010
5 Harold Wilson
6 Ken Clarke or Boris Johnson
7 Priti Patel
8 Brexiteers and Remainers
9 Senior civil servants or heads of government agencies
10 First among equals
11 (d), (b), (c), (a)

Chapter 4

1 No, judicial independence refers to the absence of political interference and influence, whereas judicial neutrality is about judges' ability to handle all cases objectively and fairly.
2 2009
3 Judges, especially those who sit in the UKSC, can be seen as unrepresentative primarily in the areas of gender, ethnicity and educational background.

4 *Ultra vires* is the term used to describe a government department or other public body exceeding its legal powers. It reinforces the notion that no one is above the law.

5 No, judges for the UKSC are appointed by a special selection commission set up when a vacancy occurs. All judges though are appointed independently of political influence.

6 EU law deals with areas overseen by the EU, primarily trade and migration between EU member states. The ECHR deals more broadly with individual human rights and tends to attract more publicity and criticism as a result.

7 Strasbourg

8 No, but it usually does. To defy the courts would be very controversial and, pre-Brexit, ignoring EU law can lead to heavy fines/questions over continued membership.

9 The UKSC must take into account both EU law and the ECHR rulings when hearing cases brought by British citizens.

10 There is no clear pattern here. Some decisions have backed the government, others have gone against it. There is no strong bias either way.

Chapter 5

1 (a) False: those in Scotland and Wales have more powers and Scotland's Parliament even has some control over income tax rates.

 (b) True: Northern Ireland not only has a different electoral system (STV), but power needs to be shared between the two communities — unionist and nationalist.

 (c) True: there have been several acts that have transferred further powers to Cardiff and Edinburgh.

 (d) False: English councils lack real legislative or tax-raising powers.

 (e) True: Scotland and Wales both use the Additional Member System (AMS) whereas Northern Ireland uses Single Transferable Vote (STV).

2 The issue that Scottish, Welsh and Northern Ireland MPs can vote on matters that affect only England, but English MPs cannot vote on the same issues that affect the devolved regions.

3 Large cities/urban areas

4 English votes for English laws

5 One from: Greater Manchester, Liverpool City Region, West Midlands, West of England, Tees Valley, Sheffield City Region and Cambridgeshire and Peterborough

6 Referendums

Chapter 6

1 Rule by the people

2 Representation, participation, accountability, legitimacy, rule of law, elections, smooth transition of power, civil rights, education and information

3 Direct democracy allows people to vote on specific questions and therefore make decisions independently. In a representative democracy, people depend on their elected representatives to make decisions for them.

4 Two from: Switzerland (initiatives), USA (initiatives), the UK (referendums and petitions)

5 Advantages:
  ● Elected representatives should be better informed on political issues than the majority of their constituents.
  ● Elected representatives may be less emotional and less swayed by populist, short-term thinking.
  ● It is faster and more efficient than direct democracy.
  ● Representative democracy protects against the 'tyranny of the majority' — representatives should consider the rights of all their constituents, not just the majority.

Disadvantages:
  ● It is not a 'pure' form of democracy: the people's wishes may be ignored by their representatives.
  ● People may participate less in politics if all the decisions are taken for them.
  ● This can also lead to feelings of disillusionment with the political system and a lack of interest in political information and education.
  ● Decisions taken without the direct approval of the people can be seen as less legitimate.

6 1928 was the first year that women and men both had the vote on equal terms. However, 18- to 20-year-olds could not vote until 1969, so you could argue that suffrage was not universal until then. If you are a supporter of Votes at 16, you might argue that Britain still does not have universal suffrage.

7 Votes for all men over 21, secret ballots, no property qualifications for MPs, pay for MPs, equal size constituencies and yearly elections to parliament

8 The Suffragists used conventional, law-abiding methods of campaigning, whereas the Suffragettes used militant action, including violence and arson. However, the Suffragettes were careful not to harm (or threaten to harm) people; they focused on damaging physical property.

9 Labour, the SNP, the Liberal Democrats, Plaid Cymru and the Green Party.

10 A move from traditional methods like joining a political party, signing petitions and attending marches or demonstrations to online methods such as e-petitions and social media campaigns. Membership of pressure groups has also increased significantly.

11 The process by which the electorate has become less strongly affiliated to political parties. This is reflected by falling party membership numbers.

12 'Slacktivism' describes the tendency for people to participate in a superficial way by 'liking' or sharing political content online.

13 Two from: Labour, the SNP and the Liberal Democrats

14 15%. This was the lowest peacetime turnout of any non-local government election.

Chapter 7

1 A plurality system. This means that whichever candidate wins the most votes wins the seat: he or she does not need a majority.

2 Votes that are not used to win seats. They include all votes for losing candidates and votes for winning candidates in excess of the number that was required for them to win the seat.

3 The tendency of FPTP to exaggerate the mandate that governments actually have. For example, in 1997 Labour won 2.5 times as many seats as the Conservatives, but only 1.4 times as many votes.

4 A constituency in which one party has a majority so big that they are highly unlikely to lose the seat in an election.

5 One in which the winner needs to have a majority of the vote to win the seat.

6 A proportional system

7 SV is used for elections for the mayor of London, directly elected metro mayors and police and crime commissioners.

8 Proportional systems are likely to create a multi-party system as seats are allocated proportionally to votes, meaning that smaller parties will find it easier to build up a presence in the legislature. Coalition governments are likely.

9 Social class: working-class voters were more likely to vote Labour, middle-class voters Conservative.

10 Age: young voters were more likely to vote Labour, older voters Conservative.

11 Labour

12 English rural areas and southern counties

13 Labour isn't working

14 It was the biggest landslide by any party since the Second World War.

15 UKIP won 3.9 million votes but only one seat in the House of Commons. This shows that FPTP punishes parties who lack geographically concentrated support.

16 May was enjoying strong approval ratings in the opinion polls, which contrasted favourably with Labour leader Jeremy Corbyn's low ratings. She (wrongly) assumed that she would win a large majority, which would allow her to negotiate Brexit with a clear mandate from the public.

17 Three: 1975 EEC referendum, 2011 AV referendum, 2016 EU referendum

18 When a government wishes to implement significant constitutional change

19 The 2014 Scottish independence referendum: turnout was 85%

20 A majority of MPs wished to remain, but the electorate voted to leave. Ultimately, parliament accepted the electorate's decision when it voted to allow the government to begin Brexit negotiations in February 2017.

Chapter 8

1 Any three from: neo-liberalism, monetarism, deregulation of business and finance, privatisation of industry, restriction of trade union powers, assertive foreign policy.

2 The third way

3 Any three from: renationalisation, increased public spending, higher taxation on the wealthy and corporations, removal of university tuition fees, a desire to avoid war or nuclear weapons.

4 Brexit

5 The Liberal Democrats

6 Labour

7 The Conservatives

8 Short money

9 Rupert Murdoch. He owns a wide range of media and both Labour and Conservative leaders have tried to win his support.

10 Jeremy Corbyn was able to increase his vote share in 2017 by relying on social media.

11 The Democratic Unionist Party (DUP)

12 UKIP: the UK is leaving the EU

13 Proportional systems

14 2010–15

Chapter 9

1 A political party contests elections with the aim of winning political power, whereas a pressure group seeks to influence those who hold power.
2 An outsider group
3 A promotional group
4 Two from: sugar tax on fizzy drinks (2018), public consultation on opt-out organ donation (2017), smoking ban (2007), compulsory seatbelts (1991)
5 2016 junior doctors' strike
6 It uses more insider methods in addition to its traditional direct action tactics.
7 Judicial review
8 A background campaign
9 Direct action
10 Labour
11 Activist lawyers used judicial review. The government's air pollution policy has been ruled in breach of the law on three occasions.
12 Someone, usually a professional, who meets with influential politicians to try to convince them to support the aims of a corporation or pressure group.
13 Pressure groups allow many different voices from different sections of society to have influence in government, allowing power to be spread more widely.
14 The Conservatives
15 Many pressure groups have far more members than the political parties do.

Chapter 10

1 The European Commission
2 The European Parliament
3 The European Council
4 The Court of Justice of the European Union
5 Free movement of people
6 The Second World War (1939–45)
7 The 2008 global economic crisis
8 The migration crisis (2015 onwards)
9 The Conservatives
10 52%
11 David Cameron resigned as prime minister and was replaced by Theresa May.
12 Boris Johnson